Mahamudra Teachings

H. E. Garchen Rinpoche

Translated by Khenpo Könchog Gyaltshen

Edited by Peter Barth

Preface

The Gar family has been renowned in Tibet for many centuries. In the seventh century, one of Garchen Rinpoche's ancestors was considered to be a great government minister for the King Songsten Gampo. During the twelfth century, Gar Chödingpa was one of Lord Jigten Sumgön's foremost disciples. In later years, Gar Tenpay Gyaltshen benefited many sentient beings by serving as the regent of the Drikung Kagyü lineage. Also Gar Chökyi Nyima was known to be a great yogi. The incarnations of Garchen Rinpoche have upheld the Dharma throughout the history of Tibet.

His Eminence Gar Könchog Nyidon Nyima Chökyi Senge was born in 1936. His Holiness Zhiwe Lodrö (the prior Chetsang Rinpoche, 1886 – 1943) recognized him to be the incarnation of Garchen Thrinley Yongchap. From the age of seven to twenty-two he stayed at the Drikung monastery called Lho Miyel-gon. At a young age he was given a special ordination during which he recognized Lord Jigten Sumgön in a portrait and said, "This is my lama." During this period his former disciple, Chime Dorje, taught Rinpoche. When Garchen Rinpoche was thirteen, Chime Dorje gave him the Mahamudra teachings. Thereafter he received all the Drikung Kagyü empowerments and teachings, started ngöndro practice, and studied the Six Yogas of Naropa.

During the Cultural Revolution there were no Dharma teachings. However, he secretly received instructions from Khenpo Münsel. With great perseverance, he practiced the teachings for twenty years. Khenpo Münsel was very pleased and said; "He is a very special bodhisattva incarnation. Of this there is no doubt."

Garchen Rinpoche is currently establishing a Buddhist College at his monastery Lho Longkar Gön for about one hundred monks. Whatever food or wealth he receives as offerings is always used for the monks and nuns. He keeps nothing for himself. He is very respectful to all persons. With loving-kindness, compassion and bodhicitta he thinks only of how to benefit others. (Background notes are taken from the article "Introducing...His Eminence Garchen Rinpoche" in the *Dharma Wheel*, the quarterly newsletter of the Tibetan Meditation Center, Vol. 4, Spring, 1997).

This text contains Mahamudra teachings given by Garchen Rinpoche during his first visit to the United States in 1997. These teachings are based on the teachings of Lord Jigten Sumgön as clarified by Rinpoche's own experience and realization and thus represent a unique record of the transmission of Mahamudra in the Drikung Kagyü lineage. In this respect, this is truly a remarkable set of teachings, stemming from the father of the Drikung Kagyü lineage.

These teachings were given in San Francisco, California, U.S.A. on July 27 and 28, 1997 and translated "on the fly" by Khenpo Könchog Gyaltshen. Khenpo is unusually qualified to translate these teachings, having authored several books on Mahamudra and the teachings of the Drikung Kagyü lineage. Khenpo Könchog

Gyaltshen has himself, on numerous occasions, given teachings in English on the subject and has also acted as a translator for other notable teachers such as H. H. Chetsang Rinpoche. His utter joy at translating these teachings for students is clearly evident even from the edited transcript.

I undertook the task of transcribing and editing these teachings, with Garchen Rinpoche's blessings, to contribute the little I could to preserving one more jewel from the land of Tibet for the benefit of living beings. As a record of the oral transmission of Mahamudra based on the instructions of the founder of the Drikung Kagyü lineage, these teachings are of immeasurable value. As a student of Mahamudra, I have found that maintaining some record of oral instructions which subsequently can be reflected upon and serve as a guide for practice to be helpful. This is consistent with the teachings of the lineage, which define the path of Mahamudra to consist of listening to, reflecting on, and meditating according to the teachings. I hope that it will serve the same purpose for other students as well.

I have tried my utmost to preserve the spontaneous flow and intended meaning of the original presentation. Nevertheless, errors are certain to enter into this process due to gaps in the recordings and my own limited abilities. To ensure accuracy of key points I would refer the more serious students to the original tapes, which are available from Ratna Shri Sangha, San Francisco, California, U.S.A. Thanks go to both Jeff Beach and Cindy Chang for recording these tapes and making them available to students.

I believe that both beginners and long-time practitioners will find much delightful and invaluable instruction embodied within these pages.

May they be taken to heart!

Peter

Introduction

The Essence of Instruction and Practice

(Day One)

First please begin by cultivating within yourselves the precious altruistic thoughts expressed by the opening prayers (see *Ratna Dharma Chakra Book of Prayers*, Khenpo Könchog Gyaltshen, 1982)

Today we will have some instructions on Mahamudra. The Buddha gave so many teachings. These are sometimes referred to as the 84,000 categories of the teachings. There is no limit to the teachings, studies and practices of the Buddha. Even if one strives to become an expert and achieve the ranks of a great scholar, one finds that there is no limit to the studies. There are countless, infinite areas of study. However, at the same time there is also the opportunity to practice without becoming a great scholar, so in fact everyone has the opportunity to study and practice this teaching of the Buddha.

When the Buddha first presented the teachings of "The Four Noble Truths," he said one should come to know the nature of suffering and avoid the causes of suffering. The Buddha taught this because every sentient being desires to be free from suffering and achieve complete peace and happiness. Yet we don't know how to become free from this suffering and we don't know how to avoid the cause of this suffering, that which is called ignorance. So the Buddha's teachings are the principal teachings which make clear how to become free from ignorance and suffering.

When we first come into contact with or try to relate to the Buddha's teachings and see the reality of our suffering, of samsara, a lot of doubts, wrong views and hesitations may arise in our mind. This is mainly due to our lack of wisdom and the power of the delusions we are subject to. Now it was in order to help us become free from these delusions that the Buddha gave so many teachings. However, since our lifetime is so short and since, within that short duration, it is so busy, it is particularly important to order our life with respect to meditation practice. It is particularly important to select a distinctive meditation practice. In the *Samadhirajasutra* it is said that the Buddha presented so many different kinds of teachings in this world and that in all of these different teachings there are such diverse levels of meaning. Yet if one gets the essence of instruction and practices that, then that substitutes for or covers the practice of all those different types of instruction and different details. That's exactly what the study and practice of Mahamudra is about. Mahamudra brings together the meaning of all those teachings.

The Stream of Realization and Transmission of Lord Jigten Sumgön

In order to bring benefits to all the sentient beings, countless Buddhas have manifested. So many beings have attained Buddhahood in the past and present. It may be said that Buddhas are countless, like the sand grains along the river Ganges.

All of those Buddhas first cultivated Bodhicitta, "the mind of enlightenment," the precious thought. Then, after cultivating this mind and gathering great accumulations of merit and wisdom and purifying all the obscurations, they attained complete Buddhahood. And with that the Buddha's wisdom and compassion was able to extend and pervade to all sentient beings. It reached to each and every individual sentient being. To accomplish this Buddha gave countless teachings.

Buddha's ultimate attainment of enlightenment is called Dharmakaya. Dharmakaya is like a space, all-pervading. Within that state of the Dharmakaya manifests the Sambhogakaya, "the enjoyment body," for the sentient beings who are known as great Bodhisattvas. Within that Sambhogakaya, Buddha manifests Nirmanakaya to reach every ordinary sentient being. So in this way Buddha's manifestations and compassion and wisdom pervade to every sentient being.

Historically speaking, Buddha Shakyamuni manifested in the world more than 2,500 years ago and gave the complete teachings. These precious teachings resulted in limitless accomplishments. For example, from Buddha, Manjushri, Nagarjuna, and so forth, and ultimately Lord Jigten Sumgön, who was Nagarjuna reborn, a lineage called the "Profound View" lineage emanated. Also from Buddha, to Tilopa and through to Milarepa, the "Blessing Meditation" lineage emanated. Alternately, from Buddha, Asanga and so forth, came the "Vast Action" lineage. This is how the lineage has come through from these great teachers until now.

Many of you know the excellent qualities of the Buddhas. The Buddha's wisdom and compassion and excellent qualities and activities are purposely manifest to benefit sentient beings. Through these precious teachings so many sentient beings have realized the supreme benefit. These teachings were transmitted through the lineage masters up until now, so these great teachers who bring these precious teachings are also in no way different from the Buddha. These great teachers gave the teachings as the Buddha did, with a pure intention, and transmitted the teachings to benefit all sentient beings, particularly those that are in the

Samsara State. So because of that, these great teachers are also manifestations of the Buddha and really no different than the Buddha.

Buddha said that his body is the Sangha, his speech is the Dharma, and his mind is the Dharmakaya. So even though historically speaking the Buddha took parinirvana and passed away and no longer exists in a human body, the Buddha's wisdom mind continues lineage after lineage in that way. Because of that many great masters or great teachers were produced in so many different places. So through Buddha's teachings, there are great teachers who studied and practiced the Buddha's teachings and actualized the Buddha's teachings by realizing the wisdom mind. So through the actualization of the Buddha's teaching, they attained the Dharmakaya. Therefore we call the precious lama the embodiment of all the Buddhas. The lama's body is the Sangha, the lama's speech is the Dharma, the lama's wisdom mind is the Buddha, because all of the Buddha's teachings are all there, are all contained therein.

When we read the great life stories of the Kagyü masters, from Vajradhara, Tilopa, until now, we can see that there were and are many great teachers. Within this lineage of great masters, today we will study the Mahamudra teachings of Lord Jigten Sumgön, the teachings that he taught and wrote. Lord Jigten Sumgön is a manifest Buddha in the human form who gave all of these precious teachings. Lord Jigten Sumgön's teachings came through the lineage from Lord Jigten Sumgön's time up until now. Like myself, each one of these lineage holders studied all of Lord Jigten Sumgön's teachings and then practiced them. So now the transmission of the teachings taught by the Buddha and Lord Jigten Sumgön will take place, here and now.

As for Lord Jigten Sumgön it is not that some of his followers are saying some great things about him which do not exist, but it is something that

Buddha explicitly prophesized in many sutric and tantric texts. Because Buddha was omniscient, knowing everything, the past and future, he clearly perceived all things without any error from within the mandala of wisdom. He prophesized Lord Jigten Sumgön's coming, the name of the place he would come from, the number of disciples, and the essence of the teachings of the Buddha. From one perspective, this is what the Buddha prophesized.

As for the lineage, when you read the life stories of the lineage masters, Tilopa contacted Vajradhara directly and was himself not different from Vajradhara. Tilopa had many disciples, but the foremost disciple and the one who could take his place was Naropa. Naropa declared Marpa Lotsawa, the great translator, to be the regent in Tibet and Marpa had many disciples. From among them the foremost disciple was Milarepa who, as we know, also had so many disciples. From among them, Gampopa held Milarepa's complete teachings, and is like the sun among all the stars. Gampopa had many, many disciples. From among them the one who held his vajra throne was Phagmo Drupa. Again, Phagmo Drupa had many, many disciples, about 80,000, and from among all of his disciples; Lord Jigten Sumgön was declared his Dharma heir and became the one who took his place on Phagmo Drupa's seat. Phagmo Drupa enthroned him as his regent. So that is how the lineage holds through these great teachers. And that's how they have the complete authority and realization of the Buddha's teachings.

In addition, it is not just the case that great teachers were limited to the 11th and 12th century in history. Recently, for example, in my monastery my root lama, who was known as the great yogi Chime Dorje, was someone who was highly accomplished and practiced Mahamudra as well as the Six Yogas of Naropa. He had lived in retreat for twelve years. Because of that his meditation and quality of practice was completed. He was so highly accomplished that there is no doubt that through him we can see how Milarepa was. In seeing him, we can realize that Milarepa was not just a myth, not just a story out of history. You can see in person what Milarepa could really be like. One can see Milarepa and other great teachers and their physical actions, verbal teachings and mental state of mind, and understand how they could do things like make footprints in rocks and move unobstructedly through walls, and so forth. So it is from this kind of great teacher that I first saw clearly and received all the precious teachings.

A Unique Juncture And Opportunity

Of those who are here today, in this particular place and in this time, many of you have come from this area, while many of you have traveled a long distance. Upon hearing about this unique occasion and due to your interest in and devotion to the Dharma you sacrificed a lot of other things to be here. It is not that we are just gathering here or something; this is something, which happened due to many causes and conditions through many lifetimes. Because of the force of these causes and conditions, through many lifetimes, we are all gathered here. Even though I don't have any great qualifications, I do possess sincere altruistic thoughts to impart these precious teachings. Thus we have come together through many positive, auspicious causes and conditions and when we receive these teachings, we should receive them joyfully and with feelings of being extremely fortunate. We should take this advantageous opportunity seriously, with the mind that not only now but also in the future we will continue to take up the study and practice of these precious teachings.

We begin by paying homage and prostrating to the precious lama who dispels the darkness within the mind of all sentient beings. The uncreated, nature of mind, uncontrived or unfabricated mind, co-emergent -- which means that it has always been within us, or the primordial wisdom awareness -- which means that mind from beginningless time has always been with us. That very nature is the nature of the omniscient. So to introduce that mind, the mode of abiding, we do so according to the teachings of Buddha in the sutra and tantra and the instructions of the precious lama. This will be done thoroughly and completely with the altruistic thought to benefit all other sentient beings. So within the special instructions to introduce the co-emergent wisdom mind of the Mahamudra, to introduce or see the mind as Dharmakaya, there are three topics: (1) the preparation, (2) the actual or main body, and (3) the conclusion, the conclusion of the way of experiencing the teachings or the enhancement through the practice.

Preparation

The Common Preliminaries

Cause and Effect

So first, even though the Buddha gave so many teachings, all of those teachings can be included in "cause and effect." Therefore we have to understand the meaning of cause and effect. Confidence in cause and effect is the root of all the Dharma teachings and the root of study and practice in the relative state.

All phenomena in samsara and nirvana depend on cause and effect and indeed everything depends on causes and conditions, whether it is something manifest or something experienced. So because of that, from this perspective, the precious human life that we have also depends on cause and effect. Since we created or accumulated great merit or good, positive causes in the past, we can call this life here and now a precious human life.

Precious Human Life

Even though there are so many human lives in the world, the human life, which we have, is even rarer still since it is accompanied by the eighteen favorable conditions. This type of life is very, very rare. It is not just rare to have the eighteen favorable conditions, but it is rarer still that we have come in contact with the Dharma teachings, directly or indirectly, by many forces. And then by contacting the Dharma teachings, we became interested in the Dharma teachings. They make some sense and we regard them to be something useful and feel, "I should do it." That is so precious. We can not get this from any other source outside of us. This kind of precious human life with a genuine interest in and genuine devotion to the Dharma teachings can not be matched by even thousands of "wish-fulfilling" jewels. The wish-fulfilling jewel is so precious but the human life, which we have, nothing else can match this. So therefore we should be confident of this and possess a clear and decisive understanding of cause and effect.

As for the precious human life, many of you have read books about this and about the corresponding eighteen favorable conditions. Just to refresh this, we will go through it briefly. When we talk about the eighteen favorable conditions, we are talking about both the qualities called the eight freedoms and the qualities called the ten endowments. The eight freedoms are as follows: we are free from (1) being in the hell-realms, (2) being hungry ghosts, (3) being animals, (4) being long-life gods, (5) being members of the border tribes, where teachings are unavailable, (6) a time in which no Buddha appeared, (7) wrong views, (8) an incomplete sense of body. There are so many human beings and of all those various beings, there are few that are interested in the precious Dharma teachings, and within that there are fewer that have time to practice these precious teachings. When we know the qualities of the Dharma teachings in a complete form, then we appreciate what this precious human life means. It becomes such a unique kind of technique or opportunity, which if we take advantage of, there is the distinct possibility to become free from all the delusions. This is something that no other life form can do. We are so fortunate to have such an opportunity to attain the complete Enlightenment State. That is what is called the precious human life.

In considering the ten endowments, there are five which we should have within us and five which we should have from outside. The five within us include (1) to be a human being, (2) the place where we are a human being is a place which has Dharma teachings to practice, (3) we have the complete sense organs, (4) we have devotion to the Buddha, Dharma, Sangha, and (5) we have not committed any of the five heinous karma. So these are the five endowments which we should have within us. And then there are the five endowments which we should have from outside. The five conditions or endowments include (1) the Buddha must have appeared in such time in which we are, (2) Buddha must have taught the Dharma teachings, (3) the Dharma which the Buddha taught has continued, that continuity of the lineage is there, (4) there should be followers of the Dharma teachings, the Sangha members, who we can take as examples of how to study, practice, follow, in the teachings, and (5) there should be kind supporters to our Dharma practices or otherwise that we have the condition to study and practice the Dharma teachings. So these five are called the endowments, which we receive from the outside.

Impermanence

So when we have this precious human life which consists of the eighteen favorable conditions and which has the complete opportunity, the distinct possibility to become free from samsara and to attain enlightenment, we must see that kind of precious jewel within our hand. So when we have this we have to take full advantage of it. If we waste it, then we have made a big mistake. We cannot ever get this again in the future. So therefore, to take full advantage of this precious human life we have to contemplate the meaning of impermanence, this momentary nature.

If we contemplate impermanence, we see how seldom it is to have the favorable conditions required to remain alive. There are so many obstacles and hindrances to life and so many opportunities for death. Even those factors or people we consider to act as protectors or sustainers of our life can become the very causes of our death. So according to the great Kadampa teachers impermanence is the most important Dharma practice to take to heart. One should reflect on and contemplate impermanence. Impermanence is such a precious teaching. At first, it gives you the opportunity to start on the Dharma path. Next, it gives you the opportunity to continue Dharma persistently without any waste. And finally, because of that, in the end it will lead us to actualize the unchanging nature of mind.

Because of that we just meditate on this impermanence and how this impermanent life just goes to the next life and then goes to the next life. In fact, we are going through life after life or we may say day after day, year after year, due to the continuity of our habitual tendencies. We just repeat the same thing everyday in our everyday life including attachment to self and hatred to those who bring obstacles. We just always go into that cycle and the cycle goes on day after day, year after year, life after life. So until we cut the rope of the continuity of the habitual tendencies which brings along endless suffering, then there is no way to be free from samsara or realize happiness.

Actualizing Freedom in Our Own Mind

In order to purify these habitual tendencies, we must practice these precious Dharma teachings, and in particular, we must practice Mahamudra. Mahamudra practice means to cut the inveterate propensity and so actualize freedom in our own mind. Right now our life is completely ruled by causes and conditions, by the so-called karma cause. We have no freedom. We don't know what will happen in the very next moment. We don't know what will happen tomorrow. This is because our life is conquered by and ruled by cause and effect that we have created.

So Mahamudra practice means to free from that, to get the real freedom within our own mind. If we cannot do that, if we just continue with this afflicted body, skandha, then it becomes like a vessel to bring all the suffering, one after the other. So when we have this skandha or heap of consciousness related to our afflicted body, we are just kind of inviting all the obstacles and suffering one after the other, endlessly, like the waves of the ocean. So therefore to free from suffering and to attain enlightenment we first make an effort to utilize cause and effect. We gather all the strength of the virtues, the causes and conditions, and avoid all the non-virtuous causes and conditions and repeatedly reflect on impermanence.

So to do these things we should realize how important the mind really is. Mind is the central figure, or the central essence, to contact and know these things and to avoid the causes of suffering and to gather the causes of happiness.

Reality and Illusion in the Duality State

If we just reflect how it is in this life we observe that we have what we may call daytime experiences and then at night we go to sleep and have dream experiences. Then the next day arrives and we wake up and again we have daytime experiences. So within this cycle, in what we consider to be our life, the daytime, we meet and have contact with people and we do things. We think and say, "This life is real." So then at nighttime, we go to sleep and dream and we say about this dream that, "This is not real." We go on like that and find ourselves perpetually going through that process.

Now when you come to die, when you go to your own death, it is as if, "This life is not real." It is now like a dream, like nothing. It does not have any essence left. And then what was the dream realm becomes real. We believe, "This is real." So bardo is like a dream, and it is real. You go through that.

So we should see how we are deluded in such a state and are dependent upon our perception, how we experience, and how the level of the mind, "real" and "not real," is the way in which we perceive in the duality state.

The Importance of the Common Preliminaries

Because of our condition, the preparatory teachings such as cause and effect and impermanence are so very important to know. Before we start the "high" teachings or reveal all the teachings – which sometimes we feel are of some other dimension – we start here since, in reality, this is where we are. Therefore Lord Jigten Sumgön said, "The preliminary teachings are more important than the actual practice." Some other teachers put emphasis on them in this way. When we know the nature of all samsara, in order to protect from this state of samsara, we should know that we have to reveal our Buddha nature and that this is the primary cause to enlightenment. To reveal our Buddha nature, we have to have the precious human life. The precious human life is indeed a special condition, a special cause, and a basis from which to know how to manifest the seed of enlightenment. Now to see that nature is so very important. The lama who knows this, who can introduce us to this, is really such a precious lama.

The Special, Proven Role of Devotion

Lord Jigten Sumgön mentioned how important it is to have confidence in the authentic, precious lama. When you have such an authentic, precious lama then with our confidence and devotion the revealing of mind is not very difficult. It becomes very easy. So therefore it is important to have devotion and confidence. Now even though I am sitting on a throne and giving these teachings, I am without many qualities but if you develop confidence and devotion then the blessings will be received not just from me but from the lineage masters, Lord Jigten Sumgön, Milarepa, and so forth. For example, there is a story where relics manifested from a dog tooth which was mistaken for Shakyamuni Buddha's tooth. It is not the dog's tooth that produces the relics, but rather they arise from the blessing of the Buddha. When you have devotion and confidence, then you receive all the blessings. So because of this reason, to have devotion to and confidence in the root and lineage lamas is very crucial, and by this you receive all the blessings. They are particularly important in order to actualize Mahamudra.

So this putting emphasis on the confidence and devotion to the lama is not something like "guru worship," but rather this is a special technique to realize Mahamudra. It is a bridge. In Tibetan Buddhism there are many lineages but, in particular, the Kagyü lineage puts emphasis on devotion to the lineage. If you read the life stories of the great Kagyü teachers you will see how much confidence the individuals have. From Vajradhara, Tilopa, Naropa, Marpa, to Milarepa, and so forth, they each have had such strong confidence and realized Mahamudra completely. They had complete realization. So even if one may not have the great fortune of hearing and studying the Buddha's philosophy, as long as one has such confidence to the teachings, to the authentic lama, then blessings arise without much effort.

Milarepa explained the reason for this when he said, "I went through great hardship. I went through all those difficulties and I crossed all of them successfully and have actualized the ultimate meaning. In the future, anyone who follows this path and just thinks of me, and just meditates, that person will not face any obstacles or any difficulties." So the lineage has come from that time until now. There is a continuity of the realized being.

This exists very scientifically in the sense that everyone knows about it and agrees to it. Also, if you read about them, it is clear that each of these great teachers, one after another, is highly accomplished in Mahamudra. Therefore we also can develop that kind of confidence and devotion to follow the path and continue this lineage. And then we can become free from our confusion and actualize the meaning of Mahamudra.

To understand the relations that may exist between the teacher, the lama, and the disciple, take the example of Marpa and Milarepa. One Westerner told me that it looks like Marpa didn't have any compassion and that he treated Milarepa so badly even tortured him. Milarepa even came to a final kind of place where he contemplated suicide. All of this was done by Marpa just to try to get to Milarepa. But in reality Marpa's compassion was so powerful. His compassion was unconditional. By knowing the whole system or the complete state and not just one small point, out of great wisdom and compassion to all sentient beings in the world, not just to Milarepa, he made Milarepa perfect. So after Milarepa went through all this hardship, one final time Marpa gave teachings to Milarepa. Marpa said, "Through the great perseverance of Milarepa there exists the heart-life of the Buddha's teachings." Because of that Marpa gave the complete teachings to Milarepa and Milarepa attained

Buddhahood within a single lifetime. And through that countless beings have benefited.

It is through Milarepa and Gampopa that the Kagyü lineage has been established everywhere in the world. Even in these days everywhere in the world people quote the example of Milarepa. For example, in the West where so many Kagyü Dharma centers have been established everyone takes the example of Milarepa and the lineage. That's how Trungpa Rinpoche and Kalu Rinpoche established Dharma centers. We are all working like this to benefit all sentient beings. So it is by the power of Mahamudra's great compassion and wisdom that we still are getting benefit. That shows how important the relationship between the lama and the disciple is to experience the precious Dharma teachings.

To have strong devotion and confidence in the lama, in the *Hevajra Tantra* it says, "Actualization of co-emergent wisdom cannot be given or explained by others. Actualization of co-emergent wisdom does not occur anywhere without dependence upon the ultimate confidence in the lama and one's own power of the merit or the gathering of the accumulations." So when you come to Mahamudra practice, it is said that the power of the blessings due to confidence and devotion to the lama, in one moment, cannot be compared to the power of the blessings due to meditation practice of the deities for 100 kalpas or eons. So therefore, supplication to and confidence in the lama is far more important than just reciting mantra and visualizing deities.

Of course yidam deities are important. They are all a part of the authentic and great lamas. For example, when Marpa met Naropa, Naropa manifested Hevajra and all the yidam deities in space so that they were visible to Marpa. Then Naropa said, "Today to which one do you want to do the prostrations? To the lama, here, where I am sitting here, or to your yidam, who is in the space in front of you." So Marpa thinks, "Oh, I see my lama everyday, but I don't see my yidam everyday. This looks like a very, very great opportunity. Today I will make prostrations to the yidam." And Naropa said, "Oh, that is not right. This yidam is the lama's manifestation" and then Hevajra and all the yidams dissolved into him. There never has been a Buddha in the past who became a Buddha without dependence on the lama. All the Buddhas of the three times manifested, attained Buddhahood through the lama's instruction.

This lama is not just the "outside lama", but there is also the "inner lama." The inner lama is as important as the outer lama, but to manifest the inner lama we depend on the outer lama. All of the 100 deities, the wrathful and peaceful ones, all of these yidams are within us, within our nature. The Buddha nature includes all of these deities. So that's why it is said that the outer yidam dissolves into the lama. We need to develop respect to both lamas but we first put emphasis on the outer lama since it is through the outer lama that we get to the inner lama. Once we get to the inner lama, at that time you realize that there is not so much difference between the two.

The Special Preliminaries

The Practice of Guru Yoga, Devotion and Confidence

All of this including the importance of devotion to the lama was explained in order to actualize the Mahamudra meaning. Now to do actual practices visualize yourself manifest as Vajrayogini, or as any of the other deities you have been practicing. If you don't know who Vajrayogini is, you don't have to worry. If you know Chenrezig or Tara or Vajrasattva, or any yidam, just visualize that to yourself. Then in the space in front of you visualize the lama upon a lion throne, on a sun and moon disk seat. Above the seat visualize lama Vajradhara. Vajradhara is the Dharmakaya of all the Buddhas. Just see this, that "my lama is in the form of Vajradhara." Regard this Vajradhara to be the embodiment of all the Buddhas and Bodhisattvas of the ten directions.

If you find it difficult to visualize, you can look at a picture first. Repeatedly just look at the picture, meditate, and then again look at the picture. I also found it difficult to visualize at first but what you have to do in any case is have confidence that this is Vajradhara and that this is the embodiment of all of the Buddha's wisdom and compassion. If you find it difficult to see all of this vividly and precisely just meditate in this way. If you can see it vividly and precisely of course this is wonderful. If you can see all the attributes of Vajradhara clearly, meditate that with the nature of great compassion he gazes at all sentient beings including yourself with a smiling and peaceful face and meditate that the lama's mind is in the ultimate meditative state of mind, which is vajra-like, indestructible.

This is important since devotion to and confidence in the lama is one of the most important factors or methods by which to experience Mahamudra or, in the case of the Dzogchen practitioner, to experience Dzogchen. When we have some genuine devotion to and confidence in the lama, it breaks all the arrogance within our mind. Even if we have such a strict and rigid mind, it gives us the opportunity to develop great compassion and loving-kindness to all sentient beings. This is a special method for gathering great accumulations of merit and wisdom. At the same time, it is a special method to purify all the obscurations. So when that kind of state of mind is there, infused with devotion, it is such a great place to experience Mahamudra. So therefore express how important that devotion is.

When you visualize the lama, make offerings. Offer the whole universe, your body, speech, and mind, as a mandala. Without expectation, offer fully your body, speech, mind, and all your root virtues to the lama. Then supplicate him from the depth of your heart, from the marrow of your bone. There are some prayers in the ngöndro text, which you can read. And then recite mantras. [Khenpo: You can say the prayers from the ngöndro text, or if you have, from the Mahamudra text.] Recite the special supplications and mantras that you have with devotion and confidence. If you recite aloud from the text, not only mentally, but also aloud in the world, it also becomes more powerful. Say, "I take refuge in the precious lama and the Buddha. Please grant me the magnificent blessing to release my self-grasping. Please give me the magnificent blessing that nothing is important to me besides the Dharma teachings. Please grant me the magnificent blessing to realize the nature of my mind, the unborn or Dharmakaya in an instant. Please grant me the magnificent blessing to become free from all the delusions. Please grant me the magnificent blessing to arise all the appearances of samsara and nirvana as the Dharmakaya." So say this prayer and do this meditation. Then meditate that from the lama's wisdom body, speech, and mind, the nectar of the blessings is received by you in the three places, the forehead, the throat, and the heart. Receive this empowerment completely, the wisdom body, speech, mind blessing of the lama, in a stream of nectar. Receive that and then let the lama dissolve into light, which in turn dissolves into you. Finally, just sit there and meditate in that state. In this state, you receive the lama's realization of Mahamudra, and it is inseparable from your mind. And it purifies and dispels the collections of all of your obscurations and negative karma that you have accumulated for beginningless lifetimes. They are dissolved and purified, right here, at this place.

So here we say the prayer, "Please grant me the magnificent blessing that nothing else is important." What that means is that, in this life, we just concentrate wholeheartedly in making the effort to gather all the accumulations. Usually we live saying repeatedly, "This is important to me," "This is important to me," "This is important to me," and because of that, at the same time we gather all the suffering. So there is so much suffering. No matter how much we could gather the things we desire, there still is no freedom from suffering. We are not freed from our suffering. In fact, sometimes the more we have, the greater is our suffering. In any case, when we don't get what we want, we suffer, and when we get what we want, we still suffer. The more we have the greater our burden becomes because of our ingrained attachment to these things. Before we get them, we fear not getting them. Once we get them we fear losing them.

It is said that it is not the things themselves that bring about our suffering, but rather it is our attachment to them. If we are free from attachment, then whether or not we have these things, there can be such a peace and happiness. Then there is no big burden. You can have such a luxurious life, without attachment, such a happy life. When you have no attachment, you are happy when you have things, you are happy, when you don't have things. This is a "broad way of happiness." So this is also a special opportunity or condition to relax your mind. Through that relaxation mind you can get a glimpse of realizing Mahamudra and through that you can enhance the realization of Mahamudra, so therefore in the prayer one says grant me the blessing so that nothing is more important to me than to actualize that.

But when we develop devotion to and confidence in the lamas, by the power of devotion, some tears come into the eyes. These are a sign of genuine great confidence in and devotion to the lama. And that becomes a special method or factor that receives the blessings. For example, when a baby cries, the mother has to pay attention. Similarly, when the tears come by the power of devotion, we are assured to get Buddha's blessings.

But that does not mean that the Buddha is not with you; he is always with you.

The blessings of all the Buddhas are always with every single sentient being. But without the condition of our devotion, it is difficult to receive the blessings. For example, when Asanga went into retreat for twelve years until he got a genuine and powerful compassion to the dawn, he couldn't see Buddha Maitreya. As soon as he got such a powerful compassion to dawn, an unconditional compassion, that served as the cause to dispel all of his delusions and obstacles which had acted as hindrances to seeing the Buddha Maitreya. At that time Buddha Maitreya said, "I was always with you, during all of these twelve years. But at this time you got to see me because of the power of your great compassion." So like that, compassion and devotion, are such a powerful factor by which to experience the Mahamudra realization of the root and lineage lama.

After receiving the blessings of the lama, which dissolve into you, then meditate in that state of the all-equipoise nature. When you are finished with this, then do the dedication.

The Practice of Vajrasattva, Indestructible Pure Being

This text includes a short Vajrasattva practice, which is the single most effective method of purification. Why do we need to do purification practice? We need to do this because it is obvious that we have some negative karma and obscurations as we are in samsara and we are experiencing all kinds of suffering. It is said that non-virtue has no good qualities but it has one quality of note in that it can be purified. If we practice purification then the fact that it can be purified becomes the one good quality of non-virtue. We got this precious human life due to the great accumulation of virtue and merit from other lifetimes. It is a result of such extremely good virtue. It is only through such good causes that we got this precious human life. Now to continue this trend in the rest of the life we need to also purify all the non-virtues and the negative karmas. Otherwise, although we got this human life through virtuous action, it is possible that this life ends with a non-virtuous action, which would not be so good. Therefore, in order to ensure that we complete this life in a virtuous way, repeatedly doing the practice of Vajrasattva becomes very important. So sometimes visualize and supplicate the lama, and then meditate and receive the blessings. And then sometimes do Vajrasattva, reflect, do the purification, and receive the blessings.

Some of you participated this past Friday in the Vajrasattva empowerment and you received those blessings. Some of you may not have. Those of you who have the Vajrasattva text can refer to this. [Khenpo: If you don't have a copy of this, our center here has the text, and if you can get that you can refer to it. Or there's a Mahamudra text too.] According to this, we will briefly explain the practice and its visualization. By this you will at least get a glimpse of what it looks like.

Visualize that you yourself as a regular person have on the crown of your head a lotus and a moon disk. On the center of the moon disk is a white HUM syllable. That white HUM syllable transforms into Vajrasattva. Vajrasattva has a white complexion, with one face and two arms. The right hand holds the vajra at the heart level; the left hand holds the bell at the waist. He is sitting in the half-lotus position, with the right leg and foot close to the front or crown of your head. He is wearing all the jeweled ornaments including the five-pointed crown, earrings, necklaces, shoulder-links, bracelets and the precious silks and robes. At his heart center within his body, visualize a moon disk. In the center of the moon disk stands the white syllable HUM surrounded by the "100-syllable mantra." When you recite the mantra, the mantra rotates clockwise radiating light as an offering to all the Buddhas and Bodhisattvas in the ten directions. From these Buddhas and Bodhisattvas emanate their wisdom and compassion and blessings which all flow in a stream of nectar to the Vajrasattva on the crown of your head. Then meditate that Vajrasattva receives this completely pure nectar. This is unafflicted nectar, which embodies all of the Buddha's wisdom, compassion, excellent qualities, and blessings. These dissolve into the HUM and 100-syllable mantra. Then the stream of nectar flows from Vajrasattva's right big toe and dissolves into the crown of your head and flows into your central channel. As it flows into the central channel it fills up all the four chakras of the body and thereby purifies all of your physical, verbal, and mental obscurations completely. Meditate that all your negative karma and obscurations leave your body in a dark smoky light from the two lower openings of the body as well as from the pores of the body. And then after purifying all of this completely your body is filled with the wisdom nectar. During this time recite the 100-syllable mantra as much as you can.

At the end of the session meditate that Vajrasattva dissolves into white light, which then dissolves into you and pervades your entire body, speech, and mind. You then manifest in the inseparable nature of Vajrasattva, in inseparable wisdom and compassion, like the vajra-bell. So meditate in such a state, in the inseparable appearance and emptiness of Vajrasattva. Then dedicate the realization of yourself to all sentient beings.

The Mandala Practice, Offering Everything

Next we have the short mandala offering instructions which are very important too. When we have a great amount of merit as a cause then it is not difficult to achieve realization of wisdom as the result. In enlightenment, emptiness is not just mere emptiness, but rather emptiness acts as the accumulation by which to get the nature of all the excellent qualities. When we make the mandala offering, that's called, "offering mandala" and "practicing mandala." As the recipient of the offering of the mandala you visualize all the enlightened beings in the space in front of you. It is not necessary to offer things that you cannot gather. Just offer whatever you have, anything, any precious jewels or precious metals. Offer anything you can put in the shrine and use this as the basis for the visualization of the offering to all enlightened beings. In front of that you visualize lama Vajradhara in the center surrounded by all the yidams, Buddhas, Bodhisattvas, the Dharma teachings, the Dharma protectors, and the lineage lamas. And to them you offer body, speech, and mind, and the whole universe, in the form of Mount Meru with the four continents, and all that. That's called "offering your body, speech, mind," or "offering the root virtue" which means something similar to taking refuge in the Buddha, Dharma, and Sangha.

Someone once asked, "If I offer body, speech, and mind to the Buddha, Dharma, and Sangha, then I have no freedom, right?" Well, that's right. No freedom to create negative karma! Because the Buddha, Dharma, and Sangha, and all of the enlightened beings, achieved such a state, they are free from all the non-virtuous actions. They have no freedom by which to create negative karma, but do have all the opportunities to gather the excellent qualities of the Buddhas and Bodhisattvas. So in this way, first visualize all of these enlightened beings as described in the ngöndro text. Go through those instructions if you want to and establish your visualization and make an offering of all that which is visible.

If we go into more detail then there are Mount Meru, and the east, south, west, north and the thirty-seven points of mandala offering. Or more briefly, one can consider the seven points of mandala offering, without any expectation, without any attachment to self make this offering, make it to the root lama, the lineage lama, and the yidams, Buddha, Dharma,

Bodhisattvas, Sangha and Dharma Protectors. Offer by saying, "May I actualize all the realization of the Buddha Vajradhara and may I become free from all the delusions. May I benefit all sentient beings through my realization of Mahamudra." That's the mandala offering. After you have done that all of the visualization dissolves into Vajradhara, who dissolve into you. Meditate that you receive all the blessings and that you free from all the attachments and boundaries. Meditate in that and then do the dedication prayer.

Do mandala offerings not only when you are sitting, but you can also make mandala offerings when you walk, even when you go to the shopping mall! [Khenpo: This is where some of you go repeatedly, isn't it?] When you see all the things in the shopping malls, instead of attaching to these things, just make offerings to all the Buddhas and Bodhisattvas. [Khenpo: Sit next to the shopping mall, sit down and say prayer... I am just teasing!]. When you go to those different stores, even the supermarket or any market, wherever you go and see things, make offerings to the Buddhas and Bodhisattvas. When you drive and see a beautiful bay, beach, flowers or people, just make offerings to the Buddhas and Bodhisattvas. Milarepa said, "Some people say I have nothing to offer. That is ignorant. Everything is an offering. Everything that you see, that you encounter, just make all things an offering to the Buddhas and Bodhisattvas." That is a special method by which to gather the great accumulations. It requires nothing. It lacks nothing. There is such a great possibility to do virtuous deeds everyplace, every time, everywhere.

The Importance of the Special Preliminaries

So the principle method or practice of Mahamudra is to release the self-grasping, the self-cherishing. So don't think that Guru yoga, Vajrasattva, mandala offerings are not Mahamudra practice. They are also Mahamudra practice. They are also teachings. These teachings are special instructions to release our attachment to the grasping of self. We always have to make this release from the self-grasping, self-cherishing the focus of any practice we do. And if we can do this, all practice becomes Mahamudra practice.

In the ngöndro text two different kinds of mandala offering are mentioned. One is longer, the 37-pointed mandala offering, the other is shorter, the 7-pointed mandala offering. You can get this from the ngöndro text. As for the supplication prayers, as mentioned earlier, "I make an offering of all my body, speech, and mind and any virtues of the three times that I have gathered here without any expectation to the precious lama. Please accept this fully." Then also offer this to the Buddha, Dharma and Sangha. Then request "Please give me the opportunity or blessing to actualize the supreme realization of Mahamudra. Please grant me the manifest blessings to give rise to the unceasing experience of the Mahamudra practice." Say these prayers to the lama, yidam, Dharma, and Sangha.

So this practice is most important for the preparation for Mahamudra. It is most important for enhancing Mahamudra practice. And finally, these are very important for the completion or realization of Mahamudra practice.

This morning's instruction has been on the preparation for Mahamudra. Is this good? This afternoon there will be teachings on Mahamudra itself. These preparatory practices are very useful since without preparation, without preparing a ground for understanding what it is about, if you just throw Mahamudra out there, there is no place by which to receive the Mahamudra. It just disappears. It doesn't make much sense. And when we get all the Mahamudra teachings sometimes we think, "It is, oh, too much." But when we first get these preparatory teachings, then when you receive Mahamudra you are more inclined to feel, "Oh, it was so useful, so very helpful, so very useful."

My explanation this morning was very brief, just enough to get the basic idea. You can read about these teachings and practices in more detail. For example, you can read about cause and effect from texts such as *The Jewel Ornament of Liberation*. It is explained very nicely in there. There are many other texts. I am sure you have read many. Read and get more. Also, there are other ngöndro practices with other ngöndro texts.

Practice

This morning we went through the first of the three topics, the preparation. We covered reflecting on cause and effect and impermanence and the importance of meditating on the lama as having the same nature as the Buddha. We also discussed the Vajrasattva practice of purification and the mandala practice as special methods for gathering the two great accumulations. Now we will begin the topic of the actual practice of Mahamudra. Here there are two sub-topics: (1) introducing the unchanging nature of mind and (2) introducing, realizing whatever arises to our mind as the nature of mind.

Introducing the Unchanging Nature of Mind

Within the first sub-topic, first there are two areas: (1) calmly abiding (shamatha) and (2) special insight (vipashyana.) In order to successfully have the special insight, the quality of calmly abiding or of mind calming, relaxing is very important. Without that, special insight is not possible. Even if you get a glimpse of the nature of mind, it disappears. We lose it right after that. So first, in order to actualize or experience that and then to sustain the special insight, calmly abiding is very important.

Shamatha, Calmly Abiding, With Support

What is calmly abiding? We need to bring our mind to the right place. That is important even in this life before we attain enlightenment, in order for us to have some happiness and peace. Also, it is very important for the mind to stay in the one-pointed state in order to be free from all the negative states. So Tilopa said, "First our mind is like a stream cascading down from the mountains. It is very fast." To simply realize "how the mind is fast and busy" is the first stage. Before that, we didn't even realize how our mind was so busy. So first look at the mind and how busy it is and have awareness of that. We have to understand how busy the mind is. It is very important to know that. In this calmly abiding there are methods called calmly abiding meditation (1) with support and (2) without support. Examples of meditating with support are bringing Buddha's image or the image of any deity to mind, or with the help of a piece of rope or piece of wood, just attending to that, or watching the breath, just focusing on it, relaxing the mind.

The meaning of this method is that the mind stays now with us. It does not follow the thoughts of the past. We often just follow or investigate what we did in the past, for example with resentment, hatred, or with attachment. We just think of the past constantly. But that will not bring any benefit at this moment since the past is completely gone. There is no use in doing this. For example, in the past someone may have hated me or "hurt me real bad" or destroyed such or such. If we contemplate on that past event, it will not bring us any benefit or any result. In actuality, it has completely left. At this moment it does not exist. So there is no benefit to resenting this or attaching to that. So just be now, in this moment.

Or sometimes we think about the future, we plan for the future. Thinking, "I will do this," "I will do that," we chase the future. We just keep chasing the future. Then, most of the time, whatever we plan does not happen. And so therefore instead of planning and chasing the future so much, do things right, right now. Gather and create good karma. Avoid bad karma.

Because the future depends on the causes that we create, if we do things right and avoid all the non-virtuous actions, if we develop all the virtues, then without planning, everything will fall in the right place. If we make a mistake at this moment and prepare such a great and wonderful plan, for example, that "we will transform all to nirvana," still it will not happen. So therefore with "not chasing the future" and "not following the past", just be now in this right place.

When mind is calm and peaceful, at that time you can see. First of all you will experience harmony and peace and at that time mind is so clear. So there is the opportunity to see, to know at that time. It is like a pond or basin or water pool. When the water is so calm, you can see what is inside. You can see what kind of bugs are there. You can see all the insects that are there. You can see what kind of dirt is there. You can see everything very clearly. However, if the water is busily churning away and just keeps on running you cannot see what is in the water. Similarly, if our mind is just running and running and running, after the past or after the future, you cannot see what the mind looks like. If we could have such a calm and peaceful state of mind, then, at that time you can see how mind is, you can see your mental position and your mental state. This is the first, most important point to realizing peace and harmony just in this life. And this is also a special cause for bringing forth the special insight.

For example, right now we are listening to or studying shamatha or calmly abiding. After receiving these instructions when you get some understanding of how to practice, then you do the practice. Of course you have heard of the seven body postures or five body postures of meditation, and so forth. Maybe sometimes it is difficult for you to have all of those qualities of body. What is important is that when you meditate you just sit with your body straight. You make your backbone straight and at the same time relax. Don't be so uptight. So with body straight yet in a relaxed position you are ready for meditation. The benefits of shamatha or calmly abiding meditation, also called the equipoised state of mind, is that when you have a good state of meditation, with mind relaxed, calm, and peaceful, that also very much helps to relax your body. When your body is relaxed and comfortable and your mental state is in harmony then your body also tends to be free from sickness and disease.

Most of the causes of suffering in this life are through the afflictive emotions or negative thoughts. The afflictive emotions or negative thoughts themselves are of the nature of suffering; they are the cause of suffering. So there is no difference between the two. We cannot say "this is suffering" and "that is a negative thought." The moment we have negative thought, such as say anger, attachment, pride, hatred, right in that place we have suffering. Right there, there is no peace. In addition, they create further suffering for us. But at the same time when you look at them, these negative thoughts and this suffering, one sees that they are just empty. No matter how much we attach to something, how much we hate somebody, the nature is emptiness. There is no essence. We get nothing except the suffering. And the suffering itself is emptiness. So therefore no matter how much we suffer, there is no benefit. We do not get any benefit at all. No matter how much we attach, we don't get much benefit. So this also shows that it is emptiness.

Due to these strong negative thoughts and afflictive emotions we in turn plant the seeds of the habitual tendencies. The more deeply we plant the seeds of the habitual tendencies, the harder they are to get rid of. They are just stuck there and it is so difficult to be free from that. We know it is not right, even intellectually we know this. But practically it is just so difficult to get away from that. We are just stuck in that. So therefore, to free from these negative thoughts which are of the nature of suffering, we need to do this meditation. Relax the mind, do not chase the future, and do not follow the past, make this kind of effort all the time. And the benefits we get from this shamatha meditation arise even in this lifetime. So if we have these habitual tendencies and if we follow them with attachment and hatred, then this causes and creates negative karma. This becomes a special kind of cause to bring suffering. So therefore, without chasing the future, just relax the mind in this state, kind of calm and peaceful.

Most of you have practiced for sometime already. As a beginner, when you first start to do these practices, when you sit down and meditate, watch all of the breath or watch the Buddha's image and relax the mind. Then you starting noticing all the thoughts, how busy your mind is. When you see how very busy your mind is and how, at that time, you cannot control or suppress the thoughts, rather than make this effort, just look at your thoughts. Don't bother them; don't be bothered by them. It is like when you come to a house and you are not the owner. There is no attachment, no hatred if something happens. If you see something which doesn't belong to you or which doesn't belong to anyone, then you just don't get bothered, you don't attach to that, you don't hate because of that. It's similar to when any thought arises to mind and you don't attach, you don't hate. There is no owner, so you just aren't bothered by the thought, you don't bother about the thought.

When we do this during our sitting, then this meditation is like when the sun rises in the morning. When there is a sunbeam or sunlight in the room, then suddenly how much dust there is! However, when there is no sun, you cannot see that in your house. But when the sun shines into your house, then how many dust particles become visible! Oh, it is so busy. So when you do the meditation, within the meditation of calmly abiding, how busy your mind is, how fickle. Your mind is so fickle. Yet don't suppress the thoughts, just let them be, and don't attach, don't hate, and relax. After all, in mind there is no one who controls that and there is no place to go.

When we do this meditation practice, start with short sessions. Sit for a very short period of time since our mind is so busy. With a busy mind, if we try to do a long session, then it may bring side effects or not much benefit. You become depressed or get upset. So to make sure that does not happen, do it for a short, short amount of time per session, with maybe 10, 15 minutes per session. Just do that, and then relax. Do that repeatedly. When you get used to it, you can make the session a little longer, and then gradually even longer. When you do this meditation practice mind should not be deluded by the duality of thoughts. This means mind should not be deluded by attachment, hatred, self and others. Be without that kind of duality-thought, and then in the non-scattered state of the mind, just practice with mindfulness, with awareness and meditate.

In the beginning, when you do this meditation, particularly when your mind is busy, it is better to gaze the eyes downwards. Gaze in the general direction of the tip of the nose, not looking too closely or too far away. Then if you are getting a little sleepy or feel like you are "sinking," gaze upwards a little. This helps to uplift the mind. Then apply this kind of mindfulness practice not only during the sitting session time but also when you walk, when you sit, when you jog, when you eat, at any kind of place or time. Your mind is always with you; maintain it in a relaxed manner. Then do all different activities mindfully, with awareness, and with relaxed state. Tilopa said, "Use many different methods to relax your mind, to bring your mind to the right place, not just one." Sometimes you need to reflect on impermanence, sometimes you may need to reflect on the suffering of samsara or on cause and effect, or maybe you need to reflect on the essenceless of mind or on how precious the Dharma is. Use all these different methods to bring your mind to the right place. So the emphasis should all be placed on how to bring the mind to the right place. This is very, very important.

Naropa got a "special method" teaching from Tilopa called "way of kind of holding the mind" method. It is like a chain, very, very complex. Apparently Naropa's mind was so wild! In order to tame it and bring it to the right place, there's a special method called "metal-like chain" which is put together in a very complex way!

So you should practice this calmly abiding meditation or shamatha until the time comes when you feel so comfortable with your meditation and you can set your mind in the right place very easily. Or, if you release that meditation, that also takes place very easily. Sometimes when you have such a meditation [Khenpo: Maybe a few, not many people maybe!], when you get such a state of calmly abiding meditation, then you feel so blissful. You feel such a peace and harmony, and sometimes you attach to that. One thinks, "Oh, I don't want to get out of this, I just want to stay there." That also is not right either. It is not right for the special insight. This kind of shamatha is very good, but if you are attached, then you cannot actualize the special insight. If that happens then you just have to break that attachment. A sign of having this happen is that when one achieves it, it is very easy to meditate, but very difficult to come out of the meditation. [Khenpo: For us maybe there is no problem with that!] Anyway, with support meditation you just have to achieve a supple state of mind. Mind becomes so flexible. When you meditate, you can meditate. When you get out of that, then you can get out of it. This is what you need to achieve. After that, then you can start shamatha or calmly abiding meditation without support.

Shamatha, Calmly Abiding, Without Support

So when one achieves this supple state of mind by applying meditation with support, then one can start with the calmly abiding meditation without support. To do so assume a bodily posture, as described earlier, in a relaxed state. Then when we do this meditation, here in the West we often have all of the things we need. In contrast, in the Himalayan Mountains when you get cold, the upper part of the body is cooler, fresh, while we may have warmer clothes on the lower part of the body. In the West you can use a heater, isn't it that so? When you get cold, there is a heater. When you get hot, then you use air conditioning. So usually, when it is a little bit cooler, that is good. When we get warmer we get sluggish, we "sink," a little more lethargy rises, things seem a little unclear. Then before long we are ready to go to sleep. So these are some of the obstacles for the calmly abiding meditation. So you can look a little more alertly with your eyes. You can be a little tenser, a little more alert. In this case, basically, your mind should be a little more alert or tense.

For example, when you have an important job to do then you have to be very careful that you don't make a mistake. Similarly, when you feel a sinking mind or lethargy, make your mind more uptight or bring up your gaze, looking slightly straighter ahead. Like that. So see, meditate by being not too tense, not too loose, just right.

You have to watch your mental position, you have to see how it is, and you have to be a witness to yourself, by yourself. When we do this practice without support that means that there is no object, there is nothing to bring to mind. Mind just relaxes in its own place. There is nothing to project, so it is called the non-objectified state. In that state, when we relax, there is nothing to meditate on, not even a dust particle. Yet, one does not scatter in any other direction. So this is a supreme kind of meditation, the mind is free from all directions.

Now when we do these meditations, sometimes we bring to them a high expectation. "Oh, my mind should be so calm and peaceful." Instead, however, your actual experience is contrary to your expectations. We expect mind to be so calm and peaceful, but instead mind is so busy, occupied with one thing after another. "How can I stop all this thinking?" You cannot do that. In the case where this happens, you shouldn't worry about that. Actually, if you are aware that your mind is so busy, that, in itself, is a very, very good quality. You are starting to settle your mind in the right place. You see how busy your mind is. This is very good.

All the business of mind, even if you try, you cannot suppress it, you cannot get rid of it, because it is just part of the mind. So just let it happen. Recognize that all of these are just part of the mind, that they are of the nature of mind. Then just do the meditation. It is good to handle the thoughts like the ocean next to us. When you go to the ocean, there are so many waves. There are tides and sometimes maybe a big tornado arises. Isn't that so? All of these are just part of the ocean. No matter how strong the tide or waves are, no matter how powerful, they are still water. They are inseparable from; they cannot be separated from the ocean and from the water. So likewise, all thoughts that arise in the mind are part of the mind. All are of the nature of the mind. So instead of pressing them down or instead of chasing them out, let them happen. Your mind remains just aware of that without chasing, without pushing. So that's a good way to handle thoughts and a good way to bring the mind to calmly abiding.

Awareness, Mindfulness and Relaxation

So when we do this meditation, with mindfulness and awareness, just be here at this moment. Stay with that. Recognize the calming of mind and the movement of the mind. When it moves, it moves; when it abides, just meditate, it is abiding. But sometimes, when we are meditating with this method, then suddenly, in between our awareness, there arises a thought. It takes place and you lose your awareness of it. It goes over in that direction. For example, you start thinking of some person, "This person is so good, so wonderful", or there is some person and you think, "This person is so bad" and that is how it goes on, with one thought after another. Then after a while you realize, "Oh, I was thinking like that!" In that state, you don't realize how you are thinking, so be very careful not to have this happen. If it happens, then in between, we create karma and plant the seeds of karma because we attach to this or hate that. With hatred and attachment, right there we create our karma! So to not let this happen, just be mindful of this moment and stay just with your thought as it rises. If you think, "This person is good" then, when this thought first comes, just let your mind relax. Don't investigate it further. What that means is don't attach to it. If a person thinks, "This is bad" then, when the thought arises, at that moment, just keep your mind aware of this thought. Don't hate, don't follow the hatred, just be at this moment. So if we can recognize all the different states of the thoughts, then we will not create karma, and this then is the way to relax.

If you are a little tired, then don't push yourself too much. Just take it easy, relax. Just relax a little bit, without thinking. Just relax and refresh your body, mind. Then you will be able to meditate so skillfully, and keep your mind from becoming too tense.

Sometimes questions may arise within such as, "What about if there are some very important things to do? Should I think about that or should I it let go?" If you think that this particular thing is very important to do, "I can't miss this, you know," and "If I let go of this, then how can I survive?" when there are some important things to think about, you just investigate it or integrate it into the practice. This means that you find a method by which to do the things within that awareness, within that mindfulness. This is important in this way; this should be done in this way. Meditate with mindfulness, without being fully involved. Meditate inside that, with that as object. Place that important item as an object and then just see all the things, which are necessary to be accomplished. As soon as we have done that and "get the idea" which we needed to get, then just continue without attachment, without hard expectation. Just do it, and then just come back to mind in the meditation state.

So in this way, as earlier mentioned, when we have a little kind of uplift or have enhanced our alertness slightly, we can become too rigid, and one gets somewhat fatigued. If that happens just relax, physically and mentally. Relax. Sometimes the body is straight, but won't relax. We have to meditate without too much ambition. So then meditate in the state of mind without bringing anything to mind. There is even no need to think, "I have to meditate." Just relax. But again, continue with your mindfulness. Do not discontinue your mindfulness. Keep in a very fresh, clear state of mind and just relax there.

Mind should be free from all elaboration. "Free from elaboration" means not being a busy mind. Mind should be in the unelaborated state, relaxed, like space. We cannot really elaborate space or the sky. Also, it is like the ocean, like the waves and the ocean, which are inseparable, which have one nature. There are no waves without the ocean. Or like the crystal, clear, all is completely clear. Or like a flower, the scent of the flower, is part of the flower. So sustain mind, fresh and clear. There are no objects to be mindful of, yet at the same time, we cannot discontinue the mindfulness. Just simply remain aware, mindful, keep the awareness. So just set the mind in that state.

Not Too Loose, Not Too Tight, Just Right

Sometimes we need to be a little more tense, uptight, then the sometimes we need to loosen, relax. It depends on the individual. Some take it so, so seriously, they are so uptight. They are tense like that. And that doesn't bring a good result either. That may bring along a side effect, like getting shoulder pains or tightness, or pressure. Those things may rise so that you have to relax and be loose always.

Some people take the instructions "relax, relax, and relax," that they become so relaxed, and then become careless. They sleep a lot and then say that they practice non-meditation. Those people need a little more alertness. They need slightly more intensity or excitement. It depends on the individual. You have to see by yourself, what is experienced in yourself.

One time a guitar player met Buddha and asked for instruction on how to meditate. Since Buddha knew that he was a guitar player, Buddha asked, "Is the sound of the guitar best when the string is too tight?" The guitarist answered, "No." And Buddha asked, "Is the sound best when the string is very loose?" "No." Buddha then asked, "How is the best sound produced from the guitar?" The guitar player said, "Not too tight, not too loose, just right." Then Buddha said, "You should meditate like that. Not too tight, not too loose, just right." Whatever is necessary for each individual.

Responsibility for Our Condition and The Power of Mind

This meditation, in one way, is so very easy. It doesn't cost anything. You just need to remain aware, keep mindfulness, and relax. Your mind is within you. You don't have to get your mind from somewhere else. It is in the palm of your hand. It is with you always, twenty-four hours a day. So it is very easy. There are no difficulties if we know how to handle things, if we know how to practice this. But at the same time if we don't know this, this "not knowing" becomes one of the most complex, most difficult occurrences. It brings along, invites all the suffering and the causes of suffering. So because of that, just meditate. First see how it is easy. "Why do I make it so difficult? I am the one who is making this difficult, no one else. Nobody else is doing this to me and no one else is causing this difficulty. I am doing this. Why am I doing this?" So meditate on the emptiness, impermanence, suffering of samsara, and suffering of the six realms.

The six realms are not something mysterious. They are very obvious and exist even in this world. We don't have to look for the hell realms somewhere else. They can be found just in this world. For example, in a volcano, there are sentient beings that are suffering so much. They are practically inseparable from the fire. This is like the hell realm. In unbearably hot weather, beings suffer. In cold weather, there are sentient beings that are inseparable from the ice. They do not die. They experience a cold hell. There are others beings like this in the world. All kinds of suffering arise due to cause and effect. This is not just something which the Buddha made up. Buddha introduced to us how the world is constituted. Due to cause and effect, we are suffering.

So look at that nature. Why am I making this so difficult for myself? I should make it easier for myself. Reflect on the delusion that we have, the kind of suffering that, because of that delusion, we are going to go through, and the causes of the negative karma, which we ourselves create. We will have to experience all of this suffering sooner or later. No Buddha will take that away from us. So see these things. And discipline yourself. Meditate. Meditate on and practice Mahamudra. When we practice Mahamudra, when we get even a glimpse of this Mahamudra meditation practice, that will destroy all delusion for 100,000's of kalpas or countless eons, and all the karma. So these are the beneficial effects of this. And we need to encourage ourselves in our own mind.

Build encouragement. Inspire yourself in these precious teachings and then do some practice, for your own benefit and the benefit of others. Nobody will be able to take that away. So just develop that kind of mind, and do this, build up this calmly abiding and Mahamudra meditation practice.

We can talk about fixation and grasping, where fixation refers to the object, and grasping refers to the mind. When the mind grasps after an object, and then that goes on day after day, year after year. That follows life after life, along with all the other habitual tendencies. Through that we experience suffering. We don't get what we desire; we get what we don't desire. We go through a lot of suffering in this way. So we should carefully, wisely investigate this. Is it right or wrong? When we carefully investigate in this way, then we see that it is true. No matter how much we grasp at outer objects, we never come to a final solution, a final happiness. It is like an illusion, like a delusion. It just appears and disappears, one after the other. So through that one sees the power of the mind.

We may utilize the power of the mind in various ways, for example, to explore the inside of the mind or to explore the outside. When we explore the mind's projections to the outside, we can create all these technologies, like nuclear bombs, which can destroy the whole world. A lot of this country does this, exploring the mind as it projects to the outside. Now if you could bring the mind's power back inside and directly explore mind and meditate, then, like all the Buddhas and Milarepa's, that kind of mental wisdom, nuclear wisdom bomb, will destroy all the delusion of samsara. It will reveal all the "pureland" of enlightenment. It will destroy all the six realms of samsara and transform them into the pureland.

Milarepa is not just an example for the Kagyü lineage but for all the lineages of Tibet. Everyone admires Milarepa's exploration of that mental "wisdom bomb" or "nuclear wisdom bomb." Because of his example, 100,000's of great teachers were produced and everyone quotes Milarepa's life story and Milarepa's songs. There is some benefit. That's why great explorer teachers do these things. And by utilizing such mental power, Buddha made great aspiration prayers and created Buddha fields. That becomes such a special place for many sentient beings to be reborn, and where they experience comfort and ease, physically, mentally. So we can see this and joyfully explore this limitless inner space, wisdom, and compassion and establish this rather than exploring outer space so much.

The Many Ways and Bodhicitta

So when we now meditate in this way, applying today's instructions on how to meditate, the importance of meditation, etc., during these times there may arise a lot of questions or even some doubt or hesitation. Doubt or hesitations, and then perhaps over joy, over attachment to these Dharma teachings. It is good to having feeling of joy and feeling fortunate, but if you attach to that and have hesitation, then you have what are called Mara. [Khenpo: How does one say Mara in English? "Mara" is something like obstacles, demons, devils] These are hindrances to progress Dharma practice and, in particular, realization. You have to dispel these obstacles.

When we study and practice these Dharma teachings, and especially when you act to uphold the Dharma, sustain it, spread it, make it available to others, generally speaking, there are three things. Because of the many different systems, individual lamas will present different explanations on how to do these things. Some put so much emphasis on study. They say you have to study this, this, this, this, and this. They believe that without doing investigations comprehensively and becoming "well studied," through studying this, this, and this, there is no way one can uphold the teachings. There are others who put so much emphasis on the practice. Of course, we have to know what to practice, and after knowing a particular subject, practice itself is very important. Through the practice one can experience realization and through that realization one can start helping others. So there are many different ways to help sustain these teachings, the precious teachings of the Buddha. So we should not have any kind of doubt about these things, feeling "this is right," or "this is wrong." All of these are wonderful ways of practice. But of all of these the most important one that we should all be aware of and which is the essence of the Buddha's teachings is Bodhicitta. Bodhicitta is the base for love and compassion. And then we should also consider cause and effect.

Bodhicitta and cause and effect are the most important and crucial teachings, without which there is no basis from which to start and no basis by which to enhance the precious Dharma teachings. There are many different examples of this. When we practice these precious Mahamudra teachings, then we may develop like Milarepa, who is well known. Regarding this, there is no doubt. There is no hesitation. This accomplishment is well known everywhere. So just continue in that way. Meditate on Milarepa and how he successfully went through so many difficulties and then actualized the importance of enlightenment, and from that state, gave the teachings. Milarepa was in a meditative state or retreat all the time until he passed away. So we, in our calmly abiding meditation practice and Mahamudra meditation practice can take that as a kind of example for ourselves. Then just do what we can in our daily life. Practice.

Vipashyana, Special Insight

Next, we begin the instructions on special insight, vipashyana. The posture of the body, the technique of the body is as before, straight and relaxed, but at this point eyes gaze straight ahead into space. Mind should be alert, clear, fresh, supple, open. When we did calmly abiding mind, mind was kind of organized, put into a certain place, with a disciplined mind. This time open the mind, make the mind spacious. So when the mind is clear and in a very clear, abiding state, look at that mind directly. Look at the mind's own nature. Then see what the mind looks like. See this carefully. See this well.

When we meditate in this way, and get the kind of decisive view or clarity. We feel, "this is it," and "there is no further to go." The mind is so clear, yet there is nothing to identify. It is fresh. So one should meditate with mind to achieve such kind of state. It is difficult to get the definitive understanding, to determine what mind looks like. One should do that meditation until one gets the definitive understanding. Until then we should supplicate to the lama and gather the great accumulations. In particular, supplicate the lama and developing devotion repeatedly. And then receive the blessings, dissolve, and just meditate there. And let all the mental activities dissolve in that state, just like the waves of the ocean dissolve in the ocean. Just like that. So when one's mind is relaxed and in its own state, with one-pointed mind, that's called calmly abiding, or shamatha. Within that relaxed, clear position, one-pointed state of mind, then look at mind itself, look at its own nature, see what that looks like. When you look at that directly, its own nature, that mind is so calm and one-pointed in nature, and there is nothing to identify and nothing to see. Yet it is an unceasing nature. There is nothing other than that. Mind is so fresh, alert, naked, which means there is no veil.

So there's something to see: that there is nothing to see. You see that there is nothing to see. You experience that there is nothing to experience. So that kind of decisive or definite kind of meaning, you get that. So when there is something really definite or final, like "there is no other than this" and yet you cannot express what it looks like, that kind of insight is called vipashyana, special insight. So there's no other place to go than this, itself. This thing is called Mahamudra.

So when we do this meditation, this is looking inside, not outside. Calmly abiding meditation, shamatha is a little inside, but still it is somewhat dealing with outside of the mind. It is not done quite fully with an inside mind. The earlier discussion was about how to meditate, how to relax the mind, how to "calmly abide" the mind. Special insight, vipashyana, is directly looking inside the mind. To do this we have to have the calmly abiding, shamatha. Otherwise, if you are without the proper calmly abiding, shamatha meditation and you want to get the instruction on insight meditation, it is like grasping space. You can't go too far, you will not be able to progress too far. So therefore look inside the mind, meditate, and get used to it as explained before. First we get the instruction, then we meditate and then we keep that meaning within our mind and sustain that all the time.

Progressing From Cascading Stream to Wide River to Vast Ocean

Progress in this practice is not a matter of going from place to place. Rather it involves exercising within your own mind and habitualizing or familiarizing yourself to this practice. Get used to it and purify the habitual tendencies of the other negative thoughts. Sometimes when strong thoughts or strong afflictive emotions arise, at that time, without that they in "force you" in one way or another, look at their nature directly. When you look at that nature directly, there is nothing to see it. That seeing there is nothing to see is called "you saw it."

With this kind of meditation the mind becomes more calm and peaceful. As mentioned earlier, at the outset our mind is like a stream cascading down from the mountains, for example, from the Rocky Mountains, so fast, so rapidly. Then, through this meditation, our mind is more like a wide river floating on the ground. Flowing so smoothly. You are aware of the movement of the mind, but it is not so powerful or stormy. Then after that, when you get used to this practice more and more, then is it like the water mixing with the ocean. It all has no place to go, it is just there. That kind of experience or meditation can arise through the continuity of mindfulness, by sustaining this practice. So at that time it is very easy to see. When the mind give rise to strong thoughts, without chasing or pushing them, you can just meditate like this.

The Great Joy of Cause and Effect

When we do these practices they may give rise to many different types of experiences. We may feel, "Oh, I have to know all these things, one has to know everything." This is something that we don't have to worry about. What we should do is be sincere to ourselves according to the Dharma teachings. Buddha gave so many Dharma teachings. So many teachings depend on the individual. Every individual has his or her own size of clothes. Similarly, in that way Buddha presented all the different teachings. In this way, he addressed beings of all different dispositions and according to all the different mental capacities. But what is really the important thing is to first see how everything arises in dependence upon the law of cause and effect. For example, meditating on calmly abiding is a special cause for actualizing special insight, and special insight is the special cause to delete delusions, ignorance. When we get this kind of understanding, experience, then one will give rise to great joy, great happiness. We see how wonderful that is and that stabilizes our mind in the precious Dharma teachings.

That kind of realization of the Mahamudra depends on the blessings of the lama. The more we have the blessings of the lama, the greater that our opportunity to experience Mahamudra realization is. So one will experience Mahamudra commensurate with one's level of devotion to the lama.

Generally in the teachings there are what are called the attainments or achievements. Sometimes you may have heard of "siddhis" or powers. There are ordinary siddhis and extraordinary siddhis. An ordinary siddhi is like flying in the sky, showing miracle powers, like the fax machine. [Khenpo: Sometimes I think the fax machine is like a miracle power, isn't it? And TV, you know.] These are called ordinary achievements. These days we use all the material things to enjoy the miracle powers. Before, in the past, people meditated inside and physically showed those miraculous powers. [Khenpo: So these days, individuals don't have to work so hard, or maybe they are working harder, who knows?] So these are called common achievements. Anybody can attain this whether Buddhist or non-Buddhist. There is another called the extraordinary siddhis or the uncommon siddhis. These are the uprooting of all the obscurations and the attainment of complete realization.

Again, so much depends on the blessings of the lama. To actualize that depends on the blessings of the lama. This is the cause of Mahamudra; therefore we put a lot of emphasis on Guru Yoga practice. Guru Yoga does not mean guru worship, but rather uniting the mind of the lama Vajradhara with our own mind, seeing our mind as the mind of Vajradhara, inseparable. To unite is called Guru Yoga. Yoga means uniting.

Unite with our own Buddha nature, do this completely and see the inseparable nature of Vajradhara's wisdom mind and our own.

Please don't feel that it is so difficult to actualize this special insight. Actualizing this special insight isn't difficulty because your mind is within you. Buddha nature is within you. You just simply need your interest, confidence, and devotion. To realize your mind is like milk and butter. Butter is always in the milk. You don't have to look for any butter, which is separate from milk. Butter is within the milk. So your Buddha nature is within your own mind. So just make it easy, and just simply follow the path.

Two Methods and the Method of Realization

Generally speaking, to realize the mind, there are two methods. One is by having great devotion to the lama, as already discussed. Sometimes there have been great Kagyü lamas who even without having been given an introduction to the mind just develop such a powerful devotion to the lama. And by receiving the blessings or by having such powerful devotion, it makes one lose one's own sense of attachment. One is fully drawn to the lama and by that power one realizes the nature of the mind. There is nothing to grasp, nothing to hold on to oneself. This is just all-pervading. In that way, the Kagyü system has such a powerful system of devotion practice.

And then sometimes in the sutras there is much emphasis on the Bodhicitta practice. By love and compassion and wisdom together we give rise to Bodhicitta. When we practice Bodhicitta, it has such a great method of equalizing oneself with others. So equalize. Then after that, exchange one's self with others and practice that others are more important than one self. And when one does this practice of Bodhicitta repeatedly, because of that power, the self-grasping, the self-cherishing, just loses. This is such a wonderful way of accomplishing benefit. There is nothing to hold on, there is nothing to grasp. There is no inner self that exists.

So then you see the inseparable nature of the emptiness and compassion. The nature of compassion is emptiness; the nature of emptiness is compassion. No separation. Realize the nature of the mind right there. So it neither exists nor does not exist. You just see that. Nothing exists independently. And yet within that, everything is manifest. You see all the sentient beings wander in samsara through delusion, without understanding or realizing these things. So of all those methods, whatever we are experiencing, realization is the most important. Without that, this introduction will not lead to any good place. So realization is the way by which to become free from the boundaries of samsara.

When we realize Mahamudra, we can find no words by which to express it. So the great Brahmin Saraha said, "When one puts a lot of emphasis or effort into organizing the mind according to the instruction of the lama, then there is no doubt that one will realize the co-emergent wisdom. And that is free from all the letters, symbols, and colors. It cannot be expressed in words. And there is no metaphor to express that." This is an embodiment of all the qualities, so how one can express it to others?

So regarding the mind which is introduced, observe that when your past mind has past, it is no longer here, and similarly, the future mind has not yet arrived, it is not yet here, and in the present moment, this moment does not exist here either. So in that way mind is free from birth, abiding, and cessation. It is so fresh, alert, and clear. That is called Mahamudra, and that is called Dharmakaya. Just look at this, just look at this moment.

The mind is free from all the boundaries. So this is a special instruction or introduction to knowing your mind, to seeing your mind.

Questions and Answers

Intellectual Understanding vs. Actual Realization

Question: "How do we differentiate between intellectual understanding and actual realization?"

Answer: Intellectually understanding is like studying a map. When you want to go a certain place, you study a map. You determine that you have to go from here to there, and then from there to here. You can see those things. This is similar to when you study and have intellectually understood something. Now when you go through that, then you don't always know what is next. So when you drive according to the map which you understood, sometimes you see that things in real are more detailed. Sometimes you see more things than you were able to pick up from studying the map. "Oh, this is different." You can get some glimpse of what it was that you understood that was right or how things are a little different. Similarly, when you study practice, you get some idea that this is how it looks like. You have not yet experienced it. You have all that knowledge in the head and maybe can express these things. But then when you practice you see, "Oh, yes, this is what this means."

Then sometimes, your experience may be a little different from that what you have studied. Up and down, back and forth, some can go through faster, some may go slower. So whether one is going slower or faster or having different experiences through the path, when you get the final realization of Mahamudra, then there is no difference. You realize Dharmakaya, Mahamudra. One's Dharmakaya is the same as all the Dharmakayas.

For example, one person may study all the maps of the world. When he has studied all the maps of the world then that person has some good knowledge, isn't that so? He has a lot in his head. We also may do that and get information about such and such place. We feel, "I must go see what is there." Then when you arrive at those places you know what kind of hotel do you want to stay at and what kind of food you want to eat and the people you want to meet. So when you do this, that is kind of experiencing it.

Of Fame and Fortune

Question: "How do you continue to strive for your dreams for fame and good fortune without attaching to them?"

Answer: To strive for fame and good fortune, create good merit and create good karma towards enlightenment. Then when you have that good merit and good karma, things will fall into the right place if you don't attach. And another thing, make whatever effort you can without bringing along attachment. In considering even how famous you might be, see how little essence there is. You can't utilize that. There is nothing there. No matter how rich you might be, you can't use everything you have. That's why there is no essence either. Let's say you owned the whole world, now what will you do? See, you can only eat one plate of food, wear one set of clothes, that much, so what is the essence there? It is just out of kind of delusion that all this arises. In reality, there is no essence. Just look at that nature and then become free from attachment.

Let's suppose you have gotten these, then when you attach to your fame and fortune they become a cause of suffering. Instead of really enjoying them, they give rise to great fear. You work so hard to protect them. You become a slave to your fame and fortune. See that nature. This is from the point of view even of samsara. Then from the point of view of Dharma practice, again there is no essence. So what we do is develop such a kind of thought, a mind to benefit others and to benefit yourself. To benefit others means to benefit to yourself. Cultivate altruistic thought, and meditate. Say the attachments to fame and fortune are obstacles to peace and happiness in the temporary state as well as the definitive state of enlightenment. In both cases the attachment to these are the real suffering.

If you read you will come across what are called the "worldly concerns." Fame and disgrace, gain and loss, pleasure and pain, honor and dishonor. So we want to achieve gain, fame, honor, and all the wealth, we don't want to get all the other four. We are just "working, oh so hard." Nagarjuna advised a king who was fully involved in those, "Don't worry about these four." Just treat all equally, so real happiness will arise, not only from a Dharma point of view but also from samsaric point of view as well.

Plow and Sky Metaphors

Question: I read a book called "Only One Blue Sky" and it's a translation of Tilopa's Song of Mahamudra, and in this beautiful book, there is a symbol of a plow and the blade. I was reminded of this when Rinpoche was teaching about being alert, in fact kind of tense, and being easy. I would like to know if the symbol of the plow were something you would associate with this practice of Mahamudra?

Answer: Of the plow and the "Only One Blue Sky", the blue sky is better. Sky has no end, no center, no fringes, no color, and also, your mind has that kind of nature.

Ngöndro and Mahamudra

Question: Is the meditation you prescribed today a practice you should be doing as you are doing the ngöndro or would Rinpoche prefer we be more advanced in our ngöndro practice before we begin?

Answer: When you are practicing ngöndro, you can also start with calmly abiding or shamatha meditation. You can do these practices one at a time or one by one. Then when you can sustain the calmly abiding meditation well, your mind becomes calmer and clearer, then in that state you may realize the special insight. That is the special insight. In the ngöndro, you have refuge, Vajrasattva, mandala offerings, guru yoga. When you do those, before each of them, do calmly abiding or shamatha meditation. Relax your mind; always put your mind in the right place. When you visualize, it is like shamatha, for example, when visualizing clearly. Then, without scattering mind in all the other direction, do prostrations and the other practices and then you are also receiving shamatha meditation. Meditate in the one-pointed nature. When that mind becomes clearer and clearer, there is also special insight, so you don't have to look for that insight separate form the calmly abiding.

The Lama of Many Lifetimes and When One Can't Find a Teacher

Question: How do you know when you have found your teacher? Is it OK to go on for years and years without a teacher?

Answer: Of the lamas, first there are two types. When you take refuge and receive Bodhisattva vows, like that, it is called the very kindness, the root lama. When you receive Mahamudra instructions from different lamas, then sometimes with such kind of lama, you just get it, "Yes, today I got the understanding of my mind through this instruction, this is it!" Some other time, no matter how much instruction you receive, it just doesn't go into your head. And other times, when you receive such instructions you feel, "Yes, I got it", that kind of flash arises like a flash of light. That is called "the lama of the many lifetimes." That is how to find the lama.

All the teachings that you get depend on the spiritual master. Without the spiritual master, we have no way to go through them. So through the spiritual master's instructions kind of helping us on the path, we progress. Then sometimes, through methods described, for example, if you supplicate Milarepa and meditate like this, then the blessings will never disappear.

There are some lamas who have many root lamas. For example, Drugthung Kunzang Gyap (?) was one of the well-known great masters. He had 500 root lamas. He counts anyone who gave him some teachings, even one sentence that makes sense, as a root lama. This is related to cause and effect, and he therefore regards such a person as his root lama.

Then if sometimes it is difficult to find a particular individual lama, then just meditate on the Buddha. Buddha's wisdom and compassion pervade to everywhere. "I am just like a blind person who cannot see things, so I take refuge to the Buddha, to all the Buddhas. In the Buddha's mind there is no difference between enlightened beings and unenlightened beings. In the Buddha's mind there is no difference. It is like when you see flowers, and all the different flowers have nectar. All the nectar is nectar." Like this. Every sentient has Buddha nature, and that Buddha nature is no different than the Buddha's, so when you take refuge in all the Buddhas and just develop pure vision then you also will receive the blessings.

When we practice these teachings, especially calmly abiding and special insight, in the Bodhisattva's path we are following, we have to practice the six paramitas. Dharma Lord Gampopa mentioned to have wealth we have to practice generosity. To receive the precious human life, we have to practice the moral ethics. To have a good gathering or entourage of disciples, practice patience. To enhance our meditation practices or achieve all the qualities of the Buddha, we have to practice perseverance. To calm our mind, to relax our mind, to organize our mind, we have to practice samadhi, the meditative concentration. And to see, to penetrate all of the realities, the nature of the phenomena directly, we have to practice wisdom awareness.

So do these practices with the base of Bodhicitta. When we do these practices, then they become a special method for gathering the great accumulations of merit and wisdom. So it is said that enlightenment depends on the collection of the great accumulations and the blessing of the enlightened lama. So when we have this kind of motivation and meditation practice, and particularly, purify our hatred and anger, the practice of patience is so important, Then follow, step by step, the path. Take the example of Milarepa who with great courage and determination, went through the practice and attained enlightenment. And through that he gave the teachings to all the disciples, so many of his disciples. All the disciples received teachings where they were. He didn't change their name. He didn't change their clothes. All of them just as they were received Milarepa's instructions and practiced and most of them achieved the rainbow body. So we just need our mental power to follow the path.

Then sometimes we find it difficult to find a good teacher. This happens. In that way we should relate to this not just for the sake of this discussion but in general, for everybody. We should separate the person and the Dharma teachings, the spiritual master, the lama, or whatever, guru, on one side and Dharma on one side. Some teachers are such sincere and great practitioners, while others we may perceive to not be such good practitioners. In some cases, when we see the mistakes of the individual, we blame Buddhism. "This is Buddhism." That I feel is not the mistake of Buddhism, but the mistake of the individual person who couldn't follow according to the Dharma teachings. So we should see that the Dharma is so precious and perfect. Because the Dharma is so precious and perfect, every single person has the opportunity to attain Buddhahood. So Dharma is so extremely precious. For each individual it is their own choice whether or not they want to follow it. But we never give up on the Dharma teachings. This is for everybody. Sometimes we misjudge an individual. Even if that person is highly accomplished because of our impure motivation and vision we may see everything what this person does as a mistake.

Not too long ago, I was in Taiwan and there was a very old lama there. During that time, one monk or priest organized a big conference on the aspiration prayer ceremony. A lot of lamas, Chinese and Tibetan, came and gathered there. So that lama, since he was so old, could not walk. So he needed someone's help to walk. So one person said he just came there to collect money! Otherwise why shouldn't he stay at his place quietly, he can't walk. So that colors people's perceptions. Now that old lama, he was highly accomplished in meditation. He was doing this to really bring benefit to all the people and to promote the precious Dharma teachings. For him, if there were one person he could help, he would just very easily stay there and help, very peacefully, without problem or making any noise about it.   Those are the kind of things we have. [Khenpo: Also in Rinpoche's case, he goes to all these different places and when people make donations and all that, he made a commitment that even if he gets one penny, he will use it to build the monasteries and to educate the monks. He made a commitment not to use it for himself, for his own benefit. Of course, when he goes around, he has to eat the food when people give it!] Therefore it's difficult to judge each and every individual.

So we should be sincere to our own self and develop pure vision to everybody, to every practitioner. Then if that lama makes a mistake, it is his responsibility. It is not our responsibility. In history, some disciples have had such a pure devotion and vision and it was their lama who made all the mistakes. When this lama died he fell into the hell realm and the disciples who had pure vision and pure devotion and confidence attained enlightenment. And then the disciple came to help the lama. So that kind of history exists.

So for our own benefit just develop pure thoughts, pure vision, and then practice Dharma sincerely because hatred and resentment are such a cause of suffering for our own mind.

Experiencing Difficulties with Rituals

Question: I feel like the part that is very difficult for me and a lot of Americans is the hand gestures involved with the mandala offerings. These are complicated. How important are the hand gestures, and so forth?

Answer: Generally these ten gestures or mudras have significance. Whether the gestures are important or not depends on the individual, and how you try to do the practice. Of course, the mind, the mental motivation, the mental, state is most important. Establish a pure motivation. With that then, if you just join one hand to supplicate the

Buddha, Dharma, and Sangha, as so precious, and develop at that place, it has great beneficial effects. There is a recent story about a butcher who always killed animals. At one time he saw Buddha Amitabha, so he raised just one hand, "Oh, Buddha so wonderful." When he died, he was reborn as a pig, but one hand was a human hand. A human-handed pig. They took pictures and advertised this widely! So understand this in that kind of way. The practice of gestures also helps your awareness, your body, speech, and mind. Somebody sometimes said that in Tibetan Buddhism there are lots of flavors, all sorts. There's meditation, there's discussion, and there are empowerment ceremonies, like when you do mandala. Like this, it helps. For example, we say "All of the universe is in my hand, now I offer this to all Buddhas and Bodhisattvas with my body, speech and mind." This kind of mindfulness. Also there are other gestures. Each and every one of these is of significance. Also, at the same time, when you feel it is difficult or boring, then first check your mind. That is important. Don't make other things more important in your mind; always check your motivation.

Buddha Nature

Mahamudra, Buddha Nature Within All Sentient Beings

(Day Two)

Good morning everybody. So the teaching this morning is a continuation from yesterday. First we cultivate the altruistic thought as we said in the prayers, to be free from the entire samsara and attain the complete enlightenment, Buddhahood. For this purpose we study Mahamudra and how to practice it. The Mahamudra nature is unstained, completely pure. The Mahamudra view does not have any rejections, any acceptance.

Because of that, in Mahamudra itself there is no path or no remedy. This is the nature of the body of all the Buddhas. This is the basis of all the excellent qualities. This is that kind of basis or foundation. It is spontaneously established by itself.

So what is this view of Mahamudra? Buddha said in the *Samadhiraja Sutra* "the Buddha nature is pervaded to every sentient being equally." So therefore there is not one sentient being who is an improper vessel. Every sentient being has the possibility, the opportunity to attain enlightenment. So now to reveal that Buddha nature, to see that Buddha nature, the Mahamudra, to attain Buddhahood, according to some of Buddha's life stories and texts may take three limitless kalpas or eons. But this depends on the individual and the path that one takes. If we study and practice Mahamudra, it may not take that long. There is some possibility of that because we have the Buddha nature and we just have to see it. So we shouldn't feel, "For me it is not possible. How is it possible for me to attain Buddhahood?" We shouldn't be discouraged but rather build courage within ourselves. "I have Buddha nature. If I make enough effort, I have the opportunity, I can do it."

Distinguishing between Buddhas and sentient beings is like the difference between clean and unclean water. What does unclean water mean? The nature of water itself is clean, but temporarily there is some stain by some chemical that can be cleaned. That can be clarified through this meditation. Therefore in Dzogchen is mentioned, "One ground, two paths, one result." This means since sentient beings have the Buddha nature, the ground of Buddhas and sentient beings is equal. To reveal that we have to take or follow into the path, and study and practice. We have to make effort with dedication, interest, and reverence to this. So this is the real path that we have to take. Then when someone attains Buddhahood, there again is no difference between Buddhahood and sentient beings. So there is one result.

So when we look at our mind, we don't look outside of the mind. We don't look somewhere else. Rather we just look inside the mind at it. We just look at that. Just find that. So when you reveal that then revealing that is called "seeing the mind", the Buddha nature. So therefore when we do this study and practice, do it joyfully, with a deep feeling of being extremely fortunate. "I have these teachings here. The Buddha nature is within me." So look at it. It is as if Buddha nature has fallen into the swamp, so just bring it out of the swamp and wash it cleanly and that's it. There is no other place to get to.

"I Think I Can"

Sometimes when you hear descriptions of the Buddha, Mahamudra is called the body of all the bodies. In the sutra system, when you read the description of the Buddha's wisdom body, it is inconceivable and has so many attributes and excellent qualities. So you find "I don't even have part of that. How would it ever be possible for me to attain that?" So when you hear this kind of thing, don't get discouraged. Generally, there will be 1002 Buddhas coming to this world during this kalpa. When you study each Buddha's life story, each Buddha has a little different quality described. Some Buddhas have more sentient beings to train; some Buddhas have less. Some Buddhas live a long life; some Buddhas live a short life. Some have a more expansive aura, and some have less of an aura. So sometimes we can think that even Buddhas have something different. Some Buddhas are bigger experts than others!

This is all according to the relative state, the relative state of the sentient beings. For example, we say the big tree and the small flowers and can explain it in this way. In reality there is no difference. This is even mentioned in some prayers, "Even the smallest dust particle contains the whole universe; and that universe is not smaller, and the dust particle is not bigger, but perfectly just there, in the relative state." So like this when you read Milarepa's life story, there are a lot metaphors, a lot of examples, which clearly demonstrate how Milarepa, through meditation practice and actualization, realized the ultimate meaning. In reality there is no difference but in the relative state all these different things are noted. So therefore we as sentient beings should not feel discouraged. "Oh, I have so far to go." Because Buddha nature is within us we don't have too far to go. It is within us. It is just a matter of meditation, putting our energy into the practice.

Lord Jigten Sumgön mentioned "As when the sun rises from the east, ask 'Does it manifest all the heat from the sun?' It doesn't. In the morning it dispels the darkness, but there is not much heat there. But when the Sun comes closer and closer to the center [of the sky] like at noon, then with it comes all the heat." So you may ask what is the difference between the sun from the east and the one at noon which produces all the heat? In reality, there is no difference. Both are simply the sun. Yet with the passage of time, it dispels confusion. Just see it. Then slowly, slowly, progress on the path and eventually it will just reveal all the qualities of Buddha. As the sun first rises in the east and then come to the noon-position and produces all the heat, so in that way we just meditate. We dedicate our life to meditation rather than say "I can't do this."

The Meaning of Sangye

Lord Jigten Sumgön quotes from Milarepa's teachings and what the great yogi Milarepa said about the Buddha regarding the meaning of "Buddha." In Tibetan Buddha is translated into the word San-gye. There are two parts to this word. First, what is the meaning of 'San?' San means fully awakened. What does 'awakened' mean? Dispelling the two obscurations. What are the two obscurations? The self-grasping, called self-grasping self, and the subtle obscurations to the omniscient. These two are dispelled and one is as if awakened from the sleep of the ignorance. That's what Milarepa said is called 'awakened', 'San'. And 'gye' means blossomed, the establishment of that which is called the self-awareness. This self-awareness clearly blossoms with the nature of the primordial wisdom. He said "I'm Mila; this is called the Buddha 'Sangye'". So we just need to dispel our delusions, the grasping to the self. We need to dispel the misunderstanding of the self to be something that exists independently and come to an understanding of that which does not exist inherently. So realize that nature. Awake from this ignorance, that kind of seed of the ignorance and realize your own nature of mind. Let the wisdom blossom. So that's called "Buddhahood," which everyone can accomplish.

Milarepa is such a well-known master. He is known everywhere these days. Milarepa's life story can be found in many languages and everyone appreciates and admires Milarepa's life and what he went through to accomplish his realization. Before that historically we have the example of the Buddha, and now more recently, Milarepa. [Khenpo: Compared to Buddha, Milarepa is more recent, isn't it? Even though Milarepa lived 900 years past!] So there is no controversy about Milarepa's life story. Everyone accepts it and takes it as an example, what Milarepa said, what Milarepa did. So this is what he said.

Even through your own experience, when you look at your mind, you can see it. It is not far. It is within you. This is not a fantasy, rather it is actual. That mind, when you look at it, is free from all the boundaries and is free from all the identification. At that level there is no subject and object, no me and you. This is empty of myself and others. There is no self-grasping, no fixation. Therefore it is called beyond the duality; it is free from duality. Like the sky of the east and the sky of the west, there is no difference. The sky is of one nature. That nature of the Dharmakaya is within every individual. Everyone has this. We just need to reveal it.

Take the example of a clay pot. The inside of the clay pot has the nature of the sky. Also when the clay pot is broken, that inner space is no different from the space on the outside. So that is called "the breaking of the clay" and is like being awakened fully. You break the clay pot of self-grasping and then you unify your mind as the Dharmakaya. This is what fully blossomed is and this is what Milarepa is saying. So Dharmakaya is all-pervading or as limitless as space or the sky.

So realizing that is called emptiness. Yet it is not a mere vacuum. We have to put so much emphasis on the compassion, which is not so easy. It is not just a mere emptiness. Compassion is so important. In Buddhism, wisdom and compassion are the most important essence of the teachings and are that upon which we have to place emphasis. Therefore it is called the "inseparable nature of the emptiness and the compassion." Where this emptiness permeates, there should be great compassion. Where this great compassion pervades, there should be wisdom, the emptiness. So to see the nature of Mahamudra, the nature of the mind that dispels the duality of the conceptual thoughts, Lord Jigten Sumgön said, "If we have not dispelled the cloud of the conceptual thoughts, the stars and planets of the wisdom will not rise." So therefore to make sure that we see the all-pervading space of the wisdom mind, dispel the cloud of the conceptual thoughts. So when we can do that, when the clouds of the duality of the conceptual thoughts are fully dispelled, then that is called Buddha, that which is within us.

Outer, Inner, and Ultimate Refuge

This fresh, emptiness awareness, the mind-as-such, contains the ultimate refuge, the Buddha, Dharma, and Sangha. When we study about refuge, Dharma Lord Gampopa said that one could differentiate between the outer refuge, the inner refuge, and the ultimate refuge. The outer refuge regards the historical Buddha to be the one who taught all the perfect teachings, the Dharma to be what he taught and what we study and practice, and the Sangha to be the followers of that precious Buddha Dharma. This is called the outer refuge. Also we could say that the lama, the highly accomplished lama, is the outer refuge. The lama's body is called the Sangha, the lama's teaching is the Dharma, and the lama's wisdom mind is the Buddha.

Then the inner refuge is within your being, within your mind, the mind that is aware and knows right and wrong. That is still a kind of Buddha. If you have studied Buddha's teachings, that "this here is right", and that "this there is wrong", seeing that is the Buddha. And application of that teaching is the Dharma. When you are applying the teachings and purifying the negative thoughts and enhancing the positive thoughts, then that action itself is the Sangha.

Regarding the ultimate refuge Lord Jigten Sumgön said that it is the all-pervading nature of your own mind, which has been pure primordially, from beginningless time, and which is completely pure by itself. That is what is called the "uncontrived" or "unfabricated" nature. We shouldn't fabricate what that means! The unfabricated nature of the mind that Buddha fully accomplished, that Buddha nature is within you. So that's the Buddha. And all the activities and manifestation from that are the Dharma or the radiant qualities of the Dharma. And that which is within the nature of that perfection is the Sangha. So there is no separation, the Buddha, Dharma and Sangha. They are explained in different ways, but their nature is one. That's the ultimate nature. So that ultimate nature of Buddha, Dharma, and Sangha, the triple-gem, is within us. So in that way we understand the relative and ultimate levels of the Buddha, Dharma, and Sangha. In Mahamudra all three are just there.

The Dharma Lord Gampopa also mentioned this ultimate refuge or Vajrayana refuge when he said, "When you realize the total nature of your mind that is called Buddha. In such a state, there is no separation between meditation and post-meditation. When you realize the inseparable nature of the meditation and post-meditation, that is called Dharma. Within that, without separation, the manifestation or display of all the activities for other sentient beings without any self-interest is the Sangha. Within that, any action you perform that is for the benefit of others is called the Sangha." So that is the meaning of the Buddha, Dharma, and Sangha, from the absolute sense of meaning of the refuge.

Mind "Free-From-Elaboration"

Then we come to what is called the "mind free-from-elaboration" or "unelaborated mind." That is basically Mahamudra. What does that mean? Sometimes the mind is free from all elaboration. It is an unelaborated mind. So actualize that state. When you think about this and then think about that philosophy and then look at your mind you feel, "How busy my mind is, one thought after another." Sometimes you feel it is not possible for you to achieve the "unelaborated mind" or be free from elaboration. "My mind is elaborating so much!" Sometimes that may make us get discouraged or depressed. We don't have to worry about that. This doesn't mean you don't think at all! Rather what it means is "don't follow after the thoughts." A lot of thoughts may arise. But when they arise, then they dissolve. Don't elaborate the first thought when you get it. If you elaborate the first thought then it describes and comments on this and that, and this is called "making elaborations." If you don't make any commentary on the first thought, just let it rise, let it dissolve, then it is called "free from elaboration." So that means you don't press the thought, you don't chase the thought. Just let that rise, let that go, and sustain your mind in the Mahamudra state. That is called actualizing the "unelaborated mind."

Sometimes, in discussing this and providing a lot of explanation on it, then that kind of adds to the confusion. What happens is that first you understand it, the unelaborated nature, and then you add a lot of elaboration to it!

Progressing in Practice

The Four Yogas

When one studies Mahamudra in detail, particularly when considering practice, one is introduced to what are called the "Four Yogas" or four stages of meditation in Mahamudra. They are the one-pointed yoga stage, the unelaborated stage, the one-taste stage, and the no-more-meditation stage. How does one identify the first stage of yoga, the one-pointed stage of yoga? When we achieve shamatha and establish calmly abiding well then at that time you can see your thoughts. At that time you can identify all your different thoughts because mind has become so calm and fine, enabling you to do that. And in that state, as you see your mind, that is called the one-pointed yoga stage.

After that, when that is well established, then as any thought arises, you just see it. Any conceptual thought that arises has no any essence. There's no essence at all. So to see that nature that has no essence at all is called "uprooting the thought." There is nothing to follow. And that realization is called free-from-elaboration or the unelaborated state. That's like the ocean and the waves. The waves may arise constantly but just each moment that they arise, they also dissolve into the ocean. A wave doesn't go to any other place. So like that, thought arises within the mind and dissolves into that, without elaborating that.

Distinguishing Between Practice and Non-Practice

There is a difference between the ordinary person's thought and the one who actualizes this state. The ordinary person gives rise to thought and then follows after the thought and then follows after the next thought, and goes on and on with this. But for the one who actualizes this state, this teaching, when thought arises, then that thought is liberated. There's no longer anything to follow. The individuals are similar with respect to the arising of thoughts. The difference between the practitioner and the non-practitioner is with regards to the elaborating of thoughts.

So when we have actualized this state, the unelaborated nature or state free-from-elaboration, then we don't follow after thought. And when we don't follow after thought, then we don't create karma or the seeds of karma. It is just like a bubble that arises in water and then dissolves. And when we have not actualized this state then, as an ordinary person, we create all the karma. We can also take the example of grass. The grass is like a thought. If the grass root is inside the ground, it will keep growing; but if you uproot the grass, then the grass cannot grow. Because it is uprooted, it ceases. Similarly, if all the thoughts arise, but you don't chase these thoughts or elaborate them, then they just cease. Each thought doesn't go far.

When we maintain that meditation all the afflictive emotions or negative thoughts, the so-called called conceptual thoughts, arise and dissolve in the Mahamudra state. And when we don't have this meditation practice, then this activity creates all the habitual tendencies, one after another. The habitual tendencies are called "the elaborated thoughts." So it's very simple in one way, you just need mindfulness. In Dzogchen it is said, "When you have the strength of sustaining the awareness and awareness is everywhere to be found, then no conceptual thought can do anything."

If we don't have that kind of mindfulness to sustain that awareness, then we follow after our thoughts. And as this way of being becomes habitualized we are engulfed in the filth of the habitual tendencies. We just repeat them one after another and we are enslaved by these thoughts.

Fanning the Embers of Practice

As a beginner practitioner, sometimes we see our thoughts and elaborate them. And when we lose our mindfulness, we cannot do the practice. So it is a matter of stabilizing the practice. When we stabilize this meditation then every conceptual thought that arises can be liberated. To liberate means to "not follow after the thought." Liberate into Mahamudra. So when we get a first glimpse of Mahamudra realization, then when smaller thoughts arise, we can liberate them. Through Mahamudra we can see their nature. But when a strong thought arises, then it may be difficult to accomplish this. A strong thought may appear to be like concrete, difficult to handle. So this is just a matter stabilizing the practice and enhancing it.

In some respects our practice is like a fire. When the fire is of a small magnitude, like incense fire, that has strength to only directly burn something small like a strand of hair. It doesn't have the strength to burn a tree. But it has the strength to burn a piece of paper or a hair. Now if you enhance that same fire, make it larger and larger, then that same fire can be so fierce that it can burn an entire gigantic tree. There is not any difference between that which burns and engulfs the giant tree and that, which burns the strand of hair. Both are fire. It is just a matter of building strength. So first we need to get the confidence through these instructions. First we get the confidence in the instruction which is without any lingering doubt. Then by achieving the confidence we accomplish the stabilization of the practice. And in that way all these negative thoughts can be deleted or demolished.

In Mahamudra practice, when we see the nature of Mahamudra, the mind as-it-is, at that time there you will see the special quality of the Dharma teachings. You will see exactly how precious these teachings are. You will see how the Dharma works and how this simple looking at mind, this single method, causes one to become free from all the delusions and to achieve all the excellent qualities. It is due to our previous virtuous deeds and the gathering accumulations of great quality of virtue that we have obtained this precious human life. All of our suffering and happiness are the result of non-virtue and virtue, respectively. All the virtues we are experiencing, all the good qualities and the happiness are due to the virtuous actions. All of the suffering that we are going through comes about due to the negative thoughts and actions, and the non-virtues. So see that nature, and realize that as a beginner we need to tame our mind by ourselves. Don't just follow along with the bad habits. Tame your own mind, if anything, because the future, your very next life, depends on this life.

Sustaining Mind, Free From Acceptance and Rejection

Whether we caste our life into the hell realm or into the higher god-like realms, we have the ability to determine this right in this life's hand. So look at that nature and remember that "just as I need peace and happiness in this life, definitely I will need peace and happiness in the next life." So by knowing that, by having this wisdom, as a beginner, we have to make effort, we make such a great effort. Then once we have habitualized or trained in our minds, then in Mahamudra practice it is said, "Free from acceptance and rejections." Even if a bad thought comes, don't feel bad about that. Even if a negative thought comes, don't feel bad about that. Just let it transcend into Mahamudra without aversion. When good thought comes, don't attach to that either. Let that be transcended into Mahamudra. So that is called "sustaining the mind, free from rejection and acceptance." So this all depends on the individual and how accomplished you are in your meditation practice.

Bringing Suffering and Confusion to the Path

So when we come to this kind of practice and when you are well established in this meditation practice, then everything can be carried or used as a meditation practice towards enlightenment. Suffering can also be used as the path towards enlightenment. At that point, suffering is no longer just suffering. There is a joy. At the beginning suffering and happiness are very concrete. They are very solid. Because suffering and happiness are a mental perception, once you learn, once you study, and once you practice, and you keep on doing this, more and more, you see that all phenomena are just a manifestation of the mind. Then suffering no longer has only the nature of suffering; it has the nature of joy. Non-virtue is no longer just non-virtue; it can have the nature of virtue. So all these things that we believe are faults or mistakes can be transformed or can be seen as good qualities. Therefore that's called all the "confusion, error dawns as wisdom."

This is the quality of Mahamudra. Mahamudra has such a great quality. The nature of everything in samsara can be seen as possessing the perfect qualities of the Buddha. So to do that, First establish dedication and confidence and then simply put effort into sustaining that through mindfulness. Mindfulness is the key to carrying all this onto the path.

An All-Inclusive Practice

When we practice Mahamudra meditation that contains all the other subjects that we have studied and have talked about. All are contained therein. When one has this awareness or the primordial wisdom, which is Mahamudra, then right there is the presence of the Buddha, Dharma, and Sangha. The glory of the Buddha, Dharma, and Sangha is right there.

When we have Mahamudra practice, this is the ultimate Bodhicitta. Right then and there one has Bodhicitta and all the peace and bliss.

In the *Hevajra Tantra* it is mentioned, "Mahamudra meditation practice contains the recitation of the mantra." When we recite or repeat mantra it is in order to transform our ordinary thoughts into the Buddha's speech. And when we visualize ourselves as the deity it is in order to purify our ordinary body. To release attachment to this ordinary body we manifest into the yidam or Buddha's body. And then to transform our negative thoughts or deluded thoughts we meditate in Mahamudra. So we do this type of meditation with body, speech, and mind to free from the cause of suffering and delusion. So when we recite any of the mantras and visualize our body as the yidam and transform things, it is similar to Mahamudra. Therefore if we have the Mahamudra state all of the time, included right there is the full presence of the enlightened states of the body, speech, and mind. That's why it is called, "This is the mantra recitation."

It is said, "This is the hardship, this is going through hardship." Why do we say "going through hardship?" Our negative thoughts, afflictive emotions are so difficult to purify and to get rid of. To do that we have to work hard. That's called going through hardship. But if we have Mahamudra practice, the Mahamudra meditation, within that no negative thoughts exist, so therefore it is called "This is the hardship practice." So in fact this does not mean you go through painstaking hardship. Rather it supercedes the hardship practice. When you have Mahamudra practice that substitutes for hardship. So you don't have to experience hardship when you have Mahamudra practice. But when you don't have Mahamudra practice, then you have to have hardship. So basically you have to renounce things to attain enlightenment. What is renounced? The negative thoughts. So when you have mindfulness on the meditation of Mahamudra, then that's the hardship.

So to purify everything, the outer, the inner, and the ultimate, and to actualize the ultimate nature, there are the Vajrayana meditation practices. With regards to this outer dimension or this outer world, to transform that, we visualize the outer mandala, the Buddhafield of enlightenment. Then, in order to purify our perception of all sentient beings, including ourselves, we visualize all as the deity. And finally to purify our negative thoughts, we meditate on Bodhicitta and Mahamudra. So when we have the Mahamudra practice, these are all included in that state. Through Mahamudra practice, we accomplish not only the ordinary achievements or ordinary siddhi; we can achieve the ultimate siddhi, Mahamudra Dharmakaya.

By reciting mantra we transcend the duality of our experience of sound. Guru Rinpoche mentioned, "The purpose of reciting mantra is to see or understand all sound as emptiness, as non-dual with the emptiness. That is why we recite the mantra of the deities." Similarly, with our visualizations, we visualize everything as vivid and empty. Everything is there, yet it is insubstantial. So when that kind of understanding and experience is present in the practice, we transcend the duality of the grasping and fixation. And that is called purification.

There is also a practice called "fire puja" or fire ceremony. The fire ceremony involves the actual burning of things in a fire during the ceremony. Why does one burn things? The true fire ceremony is the burning of delusions in the fire of wisdom. When we burn our delusions and our negative thoughts in the fire of wisdom then there arise "the four activities." Through the four activities we can burn all the negative thoughts.

First there are the "peaceful activities." Through the peaceful meditation we calm and pacify the negative thoughts. Next there are "power activities." When we overpower our negative thoughts by the meditation of Mahamudra that automatically overpowers other beings too. We can exert influence on others through wisdom and compassion. The third category is called "increasing activities." So when we enhance our Mahamudra practice then we can increase the ability of the meditation to purify, to eliminate, or to realize the nature of the afflictive emotions, and see their nature as wisdom. The fourth category is called the "wrathful activities." Through the power of Mahamudra itself, just as soon as a negative thought arises, at that very moment, by the power of Mahamudra, negative thoughts are vanquished. Mahamudra just suddenly kind of destroys or uproots the negative thoughts. Through that we can manifest activities to others to also demolish the delusions of others. So that is what is called fire ceremony.

So therefore, in a nutshell, all of these practices are included in the mind. This is how our mind can stand right where it is, how the mind can be sovereign over the whole world or the entire universe through the meditation of Mahamudra and thereby achieve all the excellent qualities.

We can go deeper into the meaning of the mandala meditations. The idea of the mandala is that it is like the whole globe or like a country or like a family and that the principal deity is like the leader of the country who at the center rules the entire country. Globally speaking, the United Nations kind of takes care of the world internationally. Or, more locally, in the family, anyone who is more powerful in the family rules that family. It is that kind of idea, which is built into the mandala. For example, in practicing Chenrezig, the great deity of compassion, whether of the 1000-armed or 4-armed form, we visualize that the whole universe is Chenrezig's mandala and that Chenrezig is at the center surrounded by the four Buddhas.

We meditate with the sense that the entire universe is outside. Actually it is all contained within our body. Our body includes the five afflictive emotions. The negative thoughts of the body are the five Buddhas, the five skandhas are the five female Buddhas, the eight consciousnesses are the eight Bodhisattvas and the eight objects of the eight consciousnesses are the eight female Bodhisattvas. They have that nature. It is not literally that. But the nature of these is the five Buddhas and eight Bodhisattvas. Or sometimes we say six afflictive emotions. The six afflictive emotions are the six Buddhas in the six realms, which are within our body. Then in the mandala we build 1002 Buddhas. When there are any of these, for example, the five Buddhas, the eight Bodhisattvas, or the six Buddhas, or the five female Buddhas or the eight female Bodhisattvas, each individual one has significance. They each have meaning with respect to the transformation and purification of our own thoughts and the duality, which we are subject to.

All of these kinds of thoughts are to benefit all sentient beings. Within the mandala there are four gates with one in each of the four directions. These four gates symbolize the four activities: the peaceful activities, the power activities, the increasing activities, and the wrathful activities. So each and every one of these activities can be utilized to purify our own negative thoughts as well as to benefit all sentient beings.

One may briefly look inside our mind with respect to how to use these four activities to purify our delusions. Through the "peaceful" means we are gentle to ourselves and to our thoughts. We uplift ourselves, bring joy, and in that kind of way peacefully purify negative thoughts. And then there arise some other kind of negative thoughts that have a little more strength. They are kind of going here or there, you need a little more power to control then. Wisdom will transform your thoughts. When we utilize this "power" activity to purify our thoughts, then that quality itself "increases" activities to purify all the delusions, negative thoughts. And in the case of the "wrathful" activities or insights, sometimes our mind is so arrogant that it enslaves you. At that time use the power of the wisdom to directly penetrate its nature and destroy that. So we have to use these four activities to purify our inner negative thoughts.

When we can do this successfully in our own mind then from that we can manifest benefits to other sentient beings. We may manifest the activities in a peaceful way. Then through power and expressing and increasing the activities of all that is good we can increase all the virtuous deeds and bring forth wisdom, compassion, peace, and glory. Those who have difficulty with respect to responding to peaceful means need wrathful actions. These wrathful actions come directly out of compassion. These are called "the four activities."

We can also relate the four activities to conventional or relative and absolute states. In the relative state it is like in a country. All of these activities are necessary in the ruling of a country. People have to have some kind of peaceful activities. When they don't listen to that we need some slightly more powerful activities, through the laws. And when that is going well, they need to increase the activities. And then, even with the law, some people may not follow them so we need policemen at the intersection, the wrathful activities. They are there to say, sometimes rather forcefully, "You are acting against the law. You are supposed to do this and that what you are doing is against the law." So even in the ruling of a country the four activities are there. And to rule our inner country, the country of the mind, we also need these activities.

There are also the four guardians who represent the four immeasurable thoughts of the immeasurable loving-kindness, compassion, joy, and equanimity.

Through this all when we manifest ourselves as one of the principal yidam deities then when we wear clothes it becomes an offering to the deity. You offer it to the deity. Regarding clothes, you have no attachment at all so you just make an offering. When you eat or drink that is also an offering to the deity. Rather than attaching to that and attaching to the taste you just make an offering. So this is to help destroy all of our self-grasping and ignorance.

As mentioned earlier with respect to the space within and outside of a vase or clay pot, break the boundary of the vase or clay pot. Destroy that. Expand the mind, and see it as the Dharmakaya, inseparable, like space.

When we do these practices then the aspiration prayers are very important. All of the Buddha's activities to benefit all sentient beings, infinitely, unceasingly, are because of the immeasurable aspiration prayer of compassion, Bodhicitta. We have to make the aspiration prayer and cultivate the motivation of compassion and the other four immeasurable thoughts. Bodhicitta is the principal cause by which to display the infinite activities and unceasing activities of the Buddha to every sentient being. So through that aspiration prayer we establish the Buddha field or the place where the Buddha abides.

So when we go through all of these studies and practice this we should understand that Mahamudra contains all of this. Mahamudra is the foundation, the ground from which everything manifests, like space. Because of space, there manifests all the planets. If there were no space, then there would be no basis by which to manifest all the planets. Likewise Mahamudra meditation practice is the foundation, the basis by which to manifest all these activities, the mandalas, and the Buddha fields.

These teachings were all taught by Buddha and it is through that great wisdom and compassion that we study and practice. These teachings are scientifically proven, whether directly or indirectly. There are so many teachings, which describe the way step-by-step and are true at the individual level such as the "nine yanas" or the "three yanas." And each so-called yana or vehicle, whatever someone may choose to study, that practice is true for that person. But that doesn't mean there isn't any place higher to go. That doesn't mean there is nothing further to actualize. So go to the higher step of Mahamudra realization.

The Three Kayas

Earlier we went through how the Mahamudra practice has all the other practices in it, including mandala offering, the fire ceremony, mantra recitation, and so forth. All that is present in the moment of the Mahamudra practice, in one moment. In this very moment, all this is there. And likewise, in the very moment of the mind in the Mahamudra state there also is present the three kayas, Dharmakaya, Sambhogakaya, and Nirmanakaya. Dharmakaya is the ultimate, realization wisdom, and Sambhogakaya manifests from that wisdom in the special body called "enjoyment body." And from that Dharmakaya state manifests the "emanation body" to benefit all the sentient beings. All three of these bodies, kayas, or forms are in that very state of mind. The mode of abiding where nothing exists is the Dharmakaya. In the mode of abiding where nothing is identified is the Dharmakaya. From that state, when all the thoughts and all the Buddha's qualities manifest unceasingly this is called Samboghakaya. And these two are inseparable. The inseparable nature of these two is the Nirmanakaya, the emanation body.

Everything arises from within emptiness. Within emptiness, the emptiness nature is Dharmakaya. Through and within that emptiness, everything manifests, anything arises, and everything is Sambhogakaya. That arising and emptiness, their inseparable nature is the Nirmanakaya. It is our mind, which does that. What if someone asks, "How do you know that, what is the source of that?" There is a quote from Buddha in the tantra text called *The Non-Duality All-Victory Tantra Text* which mentions, "The unborn nature is Dharmakaya, that unceasing is the Samboghakaya, and that which abides nowhere is the Nirmanakaya." So this is what the Buddha taught, this inseparable nature.

Even in the *Heart Sutra* [Which is popular everywhere, isn't it?] it says, "Form is emptiness." This is the Dharmakaya. It also says, "Emptiness is form." This is the Samboghakaya. And then "Form is no other than emptiness" is the Nirmanakaya. And we introduce this into the practice and understand that they are not separate from each other. They are a non-duality.

So this is a meditation practice that acts as instruction and causes for your understanding. When you understand, it is also important it to put into practice. This should not just remain intellectual. You must bring it into your heart. [Khenpo: This is my commentary: In the West we say mind is in the head. In the East we say mind is at the heart. So I thought of something. Perhaps the brain is the office of the mind and heart is the home of mind. A good compromise isn't it? Meditate here (heart) and analyze here (heart.) So Rinpoche is saying when you have understanding here (in the head) bring to just to the heart and practice.]

Practice and Establishing the View of Clarity

Now there is also self-awareness, a self-clarity. Looking at one's mind one sees nothing. There is nothing. Self-awareness, self-clarity means that there is nothing to see outside of that, outside of your mind. Look within you mind. That nature has to look at that nature, self-awareness, self-clarity. First just get a definite understanding.

Now in order to actualize that there is the calmly abiding. In the calmly abiding there is instruction on calmly abiding with support and without support. With support or without support, whatever you may be practicing, the method is to bring the mind into the right place, calm, peaceful, and in harmony. Basically, calm means harmonious. Our minds are very harmonious, possess clarity, and are in a peaceful state. Then at that place there is a great opportunity to see how it is when your thought arises. So when thoughts arise, look at that nature or when no thought arises, look at the mind. But "looking at the mind" is a thought. When thought arises, "looking at the mind" is a thought. So look at that nature. When you look at that nature, there is nothing to identify nothing to chase. Basically there is no essence. There just isn't any kind of substantial thing to hold on to. Realizing that is called "liberating" or "to liberate." So you see the nature of the liberation of the mind, and when the thought arises, there is nothing to hold on to, nothing to chase, and nothing to express. Realizing that, the penetrating nature of that, is called special insight.

With the special insight itself there is nothing to see, nothing to objectify, nothing to project. There is no projector, no projection. That is what we may experience through our meditation. And that is the kind of process we go. First we establish the view; we get the view imbued with certainty. Then that view of Mahamudra is sustained through meditation by the mindfulness. And finally, where the meditation is sustaining that view and enhancing the experiencing of realizing that, then that conduct is called the virtuous actions, free from all the non-virtues. This is called "increase or progress in the practice, step by step."

So first you must establish the view. When you establish the view there is nothing to hold on to, nothing to grasp on to. That "nothing to hold, nothing to grasp" is called clarity. The clarity nature is simply the mind's quality, free from boundaries. Just see that nature. This is how to put it into practice and to see that within one's own practice and experience.

All Within One, One Within All

Within the Mahamudra practice there are so many deities and so many mantras. But these all can be represented by one deity or by one mantra. This means that in Mahamudra, Mahamudra is such a deity of the Dharmakaya and to realize one's own nature is such a special mantra. Therefore, in a prayer it is mentioned "The Dharmakaya is like space, inseparable." That means that all the Buddhas of the past, present and future have one nature. All of their thoughts are one, all of their realizations are one, and all of their achievements are one. There is no difference. The Buddhas of the past, present, and future all realized Mahamudra. So there may be countless Buddhas, countless mantras, but they express the same meaning, purity, realization, and Mahamudra. Therefore in the teachings it is said, "The smallest dust particle can contain countless universes. That dust particle is not bigger, the whole universe is not smaller." Just freely, rest right there. This means that one Buddha contains all the Buddhas, countless in number.

Buddha said "Buddha's wisdom mind is Dharmakaya, Buddha's wisdom speech is Samboghakaya, Buddha's wisdom body is the compassionate Nirmanakaya." Now Chenrezig is the embodiment of all the Buddha's compassion, which pervades to all of the six realms. Chenrezig's manifestation goes to countless beings and comes to the one being. There is no separation between countless numbers and the one in number. Pervading to the six realms and to the one, there is no separation, there is no duality. So therefore it is said that all the victorious Buddhas are in the one dimension of the wisdom state. So therefore, for example, when you receive an empowerment, there is always the teaching, "You manifest such and such deity, now you visualize a white OM at the forehead, a red AH at the throat, and a blue HUM at the heart. From this you let light radiate in all of the ten directions and you invite all the Buddhas and Bodhisattvas into that particular deity's form and receive all the blessings." There is no contradiction between all the different types of Buddhas, deities, and yidams.

It is as if there were thousands of cows and their milk is put together and churned and we get one butter. There are thousands of cows, but all the milk and all of the butter have one nature. They are not different.

So when you study, there are a lot of different attributes, signs, signals, faces, wrathful forms, peaceful forms, different colors, white, black, yellow, red, blue, but their nature is one nature. That is called the "wisdom mind" or the Dharmakaya, which is Mahamudra. When one realizes the Mahamudra, then you'll see free from all the boundaries, free from all the fixation, free from all the rigidness. Mind is so clear, it has a kind of discriminating wisdom that is so clear and precise. There is the Mahamudra. When you realize the Mahamudra these great qualities arise. They are just there. You just reveal them.

Inseparable Emptiness and Compassion

At some point, after receiving the teachings and studying and practicing them, one comes to the inseparable nature of emptiness and compassion or the inseparability of emptiness and compassion. This is also the nature of Mahamudra. Realization of Mahamudra is the inseparability of wisdom and compassion or compassion and emptiness. To actualize that state, first we need to practice compassion with effort.

Consider all the sentient beings in the six realms. They are suffering so intensely. In particular, the cause of their suffering, the delusion, is so deep. In feeling such unbearable compassion and developing that further through effort we practice by using the six realms as an object. Through this we enhance our compassion. We project the six realms in the mind and then we practice this. And then we get the Mahamudra understanding. So practice this more and more.

Through the preceding practice you see that all sentient beings have Buddha nature. This Buddha nature is the total nature of Mahamudra. Even though all the sentient beings have this yet they have not actualized this. They are deluded. When we see this clearly then a greater compassion arises. "Oh, how they are so deluded. They have the jewel in their heart within them but have not recognized it, have not uncovered it". So they are kind of suffering helplessly. And so you see the kind of illusory nature of all phenomena and sentient beings in the emptiness state. And when that develops greater and greater that is called "effortlessly arising compassion."

The nature of the sentient beings is also empty. It is not that we are "making them empty," but their very nature is empty. In other words, the whole nature of samsara and nirvana is constituted within the institution of the all-pervading emptiness. So, as earlier mentioned, there is no object to project and there is no projector. Become free from that. That compassion is so powerful, this effortless compassion. And that is called "sustaining the Mahamudra practice." So as far as that great compassion and emptiness goes, there is no separation. They cannot be separated. We cannot say, "So this compassion over there, this is emptiness over here." It cannot be separated in your own realization, in your own experience. When you intellectually investigate them, then yes you can treat them as two things but in actuality you cannot make them two things.

In Chakrasamvara practice there are Chakrasamvara and Vajrayogini. There are two Buddhas of male and female form in union. The significance of this is the inseparable nature of wisdom and compassion. That inseparable wisdom-compassion, that very state, has a nature of great bliss and is free from all the fears. The nature of Mahamudra is that way.

Ending Karma and the Unity of the Two Truths

At this point, as a beginner when you look at mind and when a thought arises, realize its nature and it liberates itself, without any kind of remedy or antidote. Itself, look at that itself, and it self liberates. When thought self-liberates, then just sustain that. And then we don't create karma. There is no object as a basis for creating karma, there is no subject for whom to create karma, so it is called the Mahamudra state. There is no collecting or creating.

There is also no separation of the relative state and absolute state. This is called "the unity of the two truths", the relative truth and the absolute truth. Before we realize that, there is a true duality. This is relative truth. We just put it there, explain it and perceive it. Then on the other side you put this absolute truth. You perceive that and analyze that. But in your realization you cannot separate things like this. This non-duality is called "the non-duality or "unity of the two truths."

Arising and Completion

In that way, there are the so-called "arising stage" of the deity and the "completion stage" of the deity. I think that in the relative state one can say that this is the arising state of the deity while this is the completion stage of the deity. The two are separate. But in the actual practice of realizing Mahamudra this arising stage and this completion stage cannot be separated. Their inseparable nature is understood.

Without Mahamudra instruction or support for the arising of the deity, then this practice can only bring the common, ordinary siddhis. One cannot bring the ultimate, the extraordinary siddhis, which is Buddhahood. So without the sense of Mahamudra meaning within the deity yoga practice you recite mantra quite a bit and meditate on the deity form and you may establish this all through your practice. You can achieve some different ordinary achievements, such as to prolong life, dispel common kinds of obstacles, and show some different medical powers. But you may not achieve Dharmakaya. So therefore, when one practices the deity yoga and arises as the deity, whether the Buddha or any other deity, when you arise it is important to have the state of mind free from grasping, free from fixation.

The heart of the deity, the essence of the deity, is the inseparability of compassion and emptiness. So when that is not there, the deity has no life. When we are visualizing the deity with all the attributes, all the ornaments, dresses, all this, and when this meditation is going well, at the same time it becomes important to support that meditation with the view of emptiness and great compassion.

The Nature of Realization

When we talk about the realization of Mahamudra, sometimes we have a high expectation. We think, "Oh, if I have the Mahamudra realization, maybe how big that would be!" So this is like a big fantasy, like going to the mall or supermarket. But in reality Mahamudra means to just relax your mind, just rest your mind in its own natural state, to free from all the fabrication. So when you can relax in that natural state effortlessly that is called "realization of Mahamudra", "seeing that own nature."

Milarepa said, "When you talk about the view of Mahamudra, that view is your mind. Look at the nature of mind and that is the view of Mahamudra. If you are looking for a view beyond your mind, then it is like rich person begging on the street." You have all the things which are there to be had, meals and clothing, but still you go around begging. Another way to say this is it is like a beggar who has a stove [Khenpo: In the east a stove means you have two rocks and you bridge a pot on top of them, and then cook food or boil water] consisting of gold or jewels. But that beggar has not realized that and continues to beg constantly. Then one day a person comes along and realizes the situation and sees all of that gold or the jewels. He asks the beggar, "Why are you begging?" The beggar replies, "I have to beg since I don't have anything." The person says, "Your two stones are made of gold or jewels", as the case might be, and the beggar says, "Oh, I didn't know that. This has been with me for a long time. This has always been with me. I just never realized it."

It is like that. We don't realize the jewel that we have. We expect to get something from the outside. So look at your mind, realize that, stabilize that, and actualize that. And that is the Mahamudra that is within you.

In the tantra this jewel is called "the inconceivable co-emergent wisdom." The tantra text says, "Because the co-emergent wisdom is free from all elaboration, there is nothing to meditate on." Now this goes a little higher. We need to meditate. But this is explaining from the point of view of one who is more highly accomplished in the practice. At that point there is not any effort to meditate on something. But it is very important to have non-stopping awareness, mindfulness. You should always have he mindfulness of the awareness on the Mahamudra without interruption.

In this practice you don't have to worry so much about understanding or not understanding. Some people say, "Buddhism, oh, it is too complicated. You have to read so many books, complete so many studies. So I don't have enough knowledge to practice." Some people worry about that. So there is absolutely no need to worry. We just get to the essence of the practice.

Within the field of Buddhism every individual has the opportunity to study and practice. You don't have to be "smart" all the time! But the awareness and mindfulness are very necessary. So when we practice, don't worry about all those "outside" things, but rather look at the mind, establish the mind. Don't worry about so many words, but just get the meaning, the essence of the meaning. To free from samsara and attain enlightenment you have to work within the mind. Mind is the one we have to work. It is not how much you know; it is how much you purify your negative thoughts, delusions. So in that way we get free from the boundary of this life, the next life, and the bardo. Lord Jigten Sumgön said, "I, a yogin, have realized the inseparable nature of this life, the next life, and the bardo. So now I don't have to make any more effort." [If you want to read this songs, the translation is in the book called *Prayer Flags*.]

One-Taste and Impermanence

In samsara we have the expectation or hope for happiness and we have fear for suffering. But in the Mahamudra state, the nature of the happiness is emptiness and the nature of the suffering is emptiness. See that nature. That's called "one taste." Equalize that through the meditation practice. Be without fear, without attachment.

In order to do this we need to make some effort. As a beginner, sometimes we attach to this life. When we attach to this life meditation on impermanence is helpful. If we meditate well on impermanence, then at the time of death there is no fear. When there is no fear, there is no suffering. At the time of death, at that very moment, it doesn't matter how much we enjoyed this life or how much experience happened for us in this life. It is all just delusion, just illusion. At the time of death no essence is left to this. So therefore meditate on impermanence and release the strong attachment to this life.

Work on your mind to see the nature of impermanence. To see the nature of that we don't have to go to any other place, to any other dimension. You can know it right at this place, right in your home. So when we understand the impermanence, we can see that there is not so much essence to the attachment, to the happiness in this life. For all this, the mind is the principal factor. In life, it is not the number or type of objects which you have that matters. Rather it is the mind and how much you understood and actualized practice.

Practice in Daily Life and the Highway Toward Enlightenment

For that kind of practice we don't have to always depend on a retreat. You just utilize it, apply it in all of your daily life. Milarepa said, "When you walk, you just utilize these appearances as the path." This means that the appearances are vivid and clear, yet insubstantial. This is the way to walk. "When you sit, sit in the essence state." This is the way to sit. So if you have mindfulness, nothing is lacking in your practice. Even when you go to the bathroom, you can go to the bathroom in the meditative state. When you go to the kitchen, you can go to the kitchen in the meditative state. When you are driving, you can meditate driving. When there is traffic, meditate right there, in the Mahamudra state. [Khenpo: No need to honk and say "Hey you, don't block my road!" you know!]

You can use every place as a meditative state. The "four behaviors" are called walking, journeying, sitting, sleeping. Sitting includes eating. All activities are included in these. So in whatever you do, just bring awareness in the mind, instead of just talking. All talking is just idle talk. Something just comes to mind and immediately we want to express it, rather than look at it. So in that way, if we know how to do the meditation, every minute, anywhere, all the time, any place, there is the genuine opportunity to meditate. And if you don't know how to meditate, even if you go on retreat, you won't meditate successfully. So therefore, after receiving the instructions of the Mahamudra practice, put emphasis on the mindfulness.

Mindfulness is the key, the highway towards enlightenment. When we have Mahamudra practice, then even the nature of sleeping becomes evident as clarity. This clear nature is called the luminosity nature. So awareness and mindfulness, the practice of meditation, are the key to having all of these all qualities.

Inner and Outer Deities and Demons

When we have mindfulness and awareness, then the so-called deities and demons do not exist. They exist only in the duality state. Both of these, deities and demons, are a perception of the mind. And when this is understood to be a perception of the mind and you see that nature of the mind that is free from all the boundaries, that is Mahamudra. But we, as beginners, make offerings and prostrations to the deities. We hate demons, maras, and we say "Hey, get out of here! Don't follow me around." We expel them. We ask a lama to come and please expel the demons, "Please get them out!" We ask, "Lama, can you come to my shrine room and bless it?" Bringing blessing means asking deities to come. We see things in that way on the outside. We have that duality.

Then, inside we also think we have deities and demons of the mind. When we experience a bit of compassion, loving kindness, happiness, or peace, it is like a peaceful deity. We feel happy and peaceful. And then, when along comes the anger, hatred, attachment, it is like a devil or demon. It destroys our happiness and peace. So we have to recognize that. We have to see that.

One-Taste and Non-Meditation

In realization, we experience the nature of happiness as emptiness, we experience the nature of suffering or hatred as emptiness. They are equalized. This morning I mentioned the four yogas of Mahamudra, but we only covered the first two: the one-pointed nature and the free-from-elaboration or unelaborated nature. I had not yet given instruction on one-taste and non-meditation. So it is when you can meditate well, then both suffering and happiness are experienced as having the nature of emptiness. They have one taste. Meditate on that. Not rejecting the suffering, not attaching to the happiness. Whatever comes, let it come. Just sustain the Mahamudra.

When that progresses or becomes enhanced, then it becomes effortless. Then there is no need to make any effort. Then that is called "no more meditation."

So when you have this kind of practice it is similar to the following: whether snow falls, it dissolves in the ocean, whether hail falls, it dissolves into the ocean, whether rain falls, it just dissolves into the ocean. It is all of just one nature. Even if you perceive that "ah, this is snow", "ah, this is hail", "ah, this is rain", yet they dissolve into the ocean. There is no separation. Or, in other words, in the Mahamudra practice when any thought arises just see that Mahamudra nature. They are all equal.

When you have the fire of the Mahamudra, when you have any thoughts or if any complications of the thoughts should arise, put them in the fire of the Mahamudra. It burns all. You throw clothes into a fire and they burn. They become ashes. You throw trees or wood into a fire. They burn to ash. You throw all your garbage in a fire and it burns and becomes ash. Even if you throw silk into a fire, it burns. It becomes ash. When it becomes ash, there is no longer any difference. The silk is no longer special and the garbage is longer revolting. They both have become ash. So just meditate like that.

Therefore, when you meditate without grasping, without fixation, you free from the rope of fixation and grasping. There is no bondage.

Otherwise, when we have things like hatred or resentment for somebody then we always have doubt. "Oh, this person is thinking something bad about me, this person is doing something bad to me." Even if the person is not doing something like that, we have that kind of fear. That kind of doubt is always there. And there is no peace of mind. Whether that person is actual doing something or not, we always have that kind of thought. The suffering is there. So in Mahamudra, when you come to Mahamudra practice, look at that nature. For example, if someone hurts you, we perceive that person as an enemy. And when someone provokes you, then we regard this person as very provocative, right? So for Mahamudra practice, the provocative are welcome! Through them you see the weakness of your Mahamudra practice. You may say, "I know this, I understand this." You just brag or boast around here and there. Then when someone provokes you, your face is so wrenched up! You get so upset. So right there is the chance to see. Remember your Mahamudra practice, see the illusory nature, the transitory nature, the impermanence, the absence of essence. So in reality, we can say a provocative person is your supporter for the Mahamudra practice. So appreciate that. Instead of hating that person, do a prostration!

Introducing Whatever Arises as the Nature of Mind

The Essence of Conceptual Thoughts as Dharmakaya

So during all of these teachings, in addition to the description of and introduction to your mind as Mahamudra, we went through so many other commentaries. Now the second point regards the conceptual thought. The nature of conceptual thoughts is also Dharmakaya. Usually, when we have conceptual thoughts, we feel they are something bad which we have to get rid of and that non-conceptual thoughts or states are something good which we have to achieve. This is the kind of duality that we have. And with that duality, we cannot achieve or actualize "non-conceptual thought."

We have to realize the conceptual thought as having the nature of the Dharmakaya. Then, at that time, we can realize or actualize the realization of the non-conceptual thought. In order to do that, when you do meditation, with a straight body and a mind imbued with mindfulness, right in this place, right in this time, in the moment, with the mind also set in a relaxed position without movement, then just look at the mind. The mind is so clear, so fresh, as it is. Then within that state when the mind moves or a thought rises, look at the thought directly. See what that nature looks like. See the difference between the mind before the thought arises and the time when the thought rises. Look and see what the difference is between these, in their own nature. Then you realize that with regard to the nature of mind there is no difference between when it is abiding versus when it is moving. While the thought is moving, without ceasing, that nature is clear and fresh as is the mind itself. It is like when we look at the ocean and water before a wave arises and know, "This is ocean, this is water." And then when a wave arises from the ocean, we look at the wave and know, "This is also water." The water is so fresh, whether there is a wave or a still ocean, there is no difference. The wave is not separate from the ocean. Without ocean, there is no wave. So, in that nature, there is no difference.

Actions Free as the Wind and Meditation Free From Fear or Attachment

In that state, a great Tibetan king once said "When you look at the mind, mind is free from all the boundaries. It is similar in nature to space." That is the view. When you meditate on that state, imbued with the view, with mind free from all the boundaries and with a nature like space, then the luminosity mind is also right there, like the sun and moon. In that state, when you meditate and perform actions with non-attachment, non-hatred, it is like riding on the wind. Wind flows everywhere. It is not attached to anything. It has no hatred to anything. Whether there is a clean place or a dirty place, it just goes there. It has no hatred to the dirty place. It does not attach to the clean place.

So at this time when you meditate, when you actualize this, the thoughts are just the manifestations of the mind. Whether a thought is positive or negative, there is complete non-attachment to these different types of thoughts. The thought cannot do anything for or to you. The thought cannot benefit you. The thought cannot harm you. That is called "free from all the fear or attachment".

Do this meditation for perhaps one hour. First visualize Milarepa or the other great teachers, and supplicate them, ask for their support and receive their blessings. Let them dissolve into you. Meditate in Mahamudra, mixing, unifying your mind with this enlightened teacher, and experience this and just relax there. And then, at the end of the meditation, do the dedication. So do these practices, one hour, or half-an hour, or two hours, whatever time you have.

No matter how powerful the waves may be, still water is part of the ocean. Likewise, no matter how powerful thoughts may be, they are still part of the mind. Without pushing or chasing thoughts, see that nature. It is just like seeing that the waves are of the nature of the ocean. A wave is no other than the ocean, the ocean no other than the wave. The wave arises from the ocean and dissolves into the ocean. So, in the unchanging nature of the mind, within that clarity state, whatever different type of thought arises, don't separate these two, this inseparable nature. Just relax in that.

In the *Hevajra Tantra* it is said, "When you don't realize the nature of thought, when you don't know thought, that thought becomes very independent and powerful, and is called samsara. When you realize the nature of the thought, without any pushing or chasing and see its self-nature directly, that is called nirvana." So therefore there is no nirvana that exists separately from samsara.

So in this context, realizing the conceptual thought as the Dharmakaya, as noted earlier, when we recognize the thought as soon as the thought arises, and see that nature as emptiness and that it is no different from the mind, that is called liberation. It is liberated. It has no power. Thought no longer creates karma. On the other hand, when thought arises and you just follow into it and habitualize the thought and the following, the seeds of the habitual tendencies are planted so deeply, and that is called creating karma. That is called samsara. So this one thought, when you realize its nature, then there is nirvana, and it is liberated. And that very thought, when it is not liberated and not seen by Mahamudra, and we just follow that thought into duality, with attachment and hatred, it creates all the karma and becomes samsara.

Mindfulness and Meditation Sessions

I would like to emphasize that when you meditate, practice mindfulness and awareness, and stay with that. It becomes easier, and easier, and easier to do this kind of practice. So do those kinds of sessions. For example, bring mindfulness, first, say, three or four times during a meditation session. Doing a meditation session is the method by which to bring mindfulness repeatedly. Sometimes you can write notes to yourself and place them in the rooms of your home, "mindfulness," "mindfulness," you know, to remind yourself. You can write a piece of paper that says "mindfulness" and put it in the bathroom. Like that!

Sometime some yogis had long hair on their head, they put something special there and then when it shows up in front of their eyes, they remember "this is for mindfulness." First design practice like that. As soon as it comes in sight, "Oh, now comes back the mindfulness!" Or you could make a difficult step to your door, instead of making it so comfortable. "When I come to this, I just bring my mindfulness there. I designed this in the first place for reminding me like that." So refreshing mindfulness is very, very important.

Confusion Dawning as Wisdom

Even though we may have Mahamudra view and understanding quite well, without mindfulness it doesn't do us any good. It is again hidden there. It is not with us. So we always have to have mindfulness. When a thought arises, immediately it just dissolves. This is called "thought arises and then dissolve without trace." Without a trace, with no root. In

Dzogchen there is a saying, "It is like drawing on the water." When you draw on the water, when you are drawing, what happens? It dissolves, doesn't it? Your thought arises, dissolves into the water of the Mahamudra. When you are drawing your thoughts, on the water of the Mahamudra, then it dissolves right there. So that is called "liberating the conceptual thoughts into Dharmakaya." It is called "Dawning the confusion as the wisdom, Dharmakaya."

This is the kind of mindfulness we have to sustain through all our conduct and activities. This is called mindfulness, awareness, and vigilance. Notice that when you come to a gathering of people, at that time, you are a little tenser. This is a kind of tense time for your mindfulness. At that time, say to yourself, "I should be more mindful, make it stronger." Then when you are alone, relax. Look at the freshness of the mind. So these are the methods, first to realize, to recognize our conceptual thought as the Dharmakaya, which is no different from the mind and how to sustain that meditation.

"To Realize or Not to Realize"

So in this practice, in Mahamudra, there are some different analogies with regards to realizing the nature of the conceptual thoughts or not realizing it successfully.

First of all, this realizing thought as Dharmakaya in just one moment is called "instant enlightenment." If you know that, you know. If you want instant enlightenment, look at the thought, and see its nature as Dharmakaya, and there is instant enlightenment. So you don't have to go to any other place. Just right at your own seat, directly get that instant enlightenment! But if you don't realize that as the Dharmakaya, then it is "instant samsara!" So samsara is never too far away either. It is just an instant away.

In Mahamudra there is also the example of gold and sand. Just as soon as you realize your conceptual thought as the Dharmakaya, then that thought is like gold, so extremely precious. But if you don't realize the thought as the Dharmakaya, then it is like the sand. It is not at all precious. Or, when you realize your thoughts, it is like water and ice. Our mind and thoughts are like frozen water or ice and Buddha's mind is like water. So as soon as we realize our thoughts as the Dharmakaya, they melt into water. As long as it stays as ordinary conceptual thought, it is ice. Therefore, in this the devotion to or confidence in the lama becomes very important. The devotion and compassion are principal factors by which to melt the frozen or freezing mind into the water of the Dharmakaya. That's why, Lord Jigten Sumgön mentioned, in the song *The Fivefold Profound Path of Mahamudra* that "If the sun of the devotion doesn't shine on the snow mountain of the four kayas of the lama then the stream of the blessings will not be received. Therefore be sure of the importance of this devotion." As soon as one has strong devotion or great compassion, then the thought melts by the fire of Mahamudra, into the ocean of Dharmakaya.

In Dzogchen an example is given about our conceptual thought, "When we have not realized it as the Dharmakaya, it is like water dropped into the dust and mixed with the dust which becomes mud". We cannot separate the mud and the water, the nature of samsara. But it then goes on to say, "As soon as you realize your conceptual thoughts as the Dharmakaya, it is like mercury." No matter how hard you drop mercury onto dust, it does not mix with the dust. No matter how much it goes into pieces, it all remains independent and pure. That doesn't affect it. Like that.

So samsara is like the freezer, when you put water into the freezer, it turns into ice. All our thoughts are turned into the conceptual thoughts, duality, and become samsara. And this Mahamudra is like a fire. As soon as the thought arises, meditate on the Mahamudra, it dissolves into Dharmakaya and becomes nirvana.

The Luminosity of Great Bliss

There is one point. Whether the conceptual thought is liberated into the Dharmakaya or is samsara, when you see your mind, the thought dissolves into Dharmakaya. At that point there arises some kind of joy, a real joy. You don't know where it comes from. You don't know what the cause of that is but there is some joy, some bliss there. So that is the sign that your conceptual thought has dissolved into the Dharmakaya or the Mahamudra, in one moment.

In the case where one conceptual thought dissolves into the Dharmakaya or Mahamudra and there is that kind of bliss and joy, then, of course, if you have the continuity of that meditation any thought that arises dissolves into this Mahamudra state. As any thought is recognized as having the nature of Mahamudra, then, of course, there is this great joy. This is called "the great joy of clarity or luminosity" or "the luminosity of the great joy. " That joy is free of all fear.

The mind becomes very broad and spacious, with a nature like space, and one can see all very clearly, without any kind of mistake. It is like when you look from here and see all persons at one time. When we don't have that, when the mind is kind of narrow and the conceptual thoughts are not realized as having the Mahamudra nature, then mind is narrow. It is like looking just at one person. When you look at one person, you miss seeing every other person in the hall. For example, you meet somebody there and you just get completely involved in talking or discussing something there. Then you have no idea or sense of what is happening in the hall. So the clarity nature means "clearness". It is so spacious, without obstruction. You see very clearly, vividly, precisely. That is called "the clarity" and since there is no fear, it is also just called "great joy."

The Five Wisdoms

In the earlier instruction on the practice of meditation, we discussed the example of the fire of one stick of incense in contrast to a big forest fire. You may read and write many things, but these all remain outside. Take them to heart, inside the mind, this experience. When you have the experience of the Mahamudra, our small experience of the Mahamudra practice is like the incense fire. It can burn paper or something small like that. Then when that becomes stronger and stronger, like a raging fire storm, then all kind of solid things can burn in that too. So the main point of all is just to look, watch. Watch the nature of the conceptual thoughts. Just look at that. When thoughts arise, without chasing, pushing, just look at that nature and sustain that.

When we do this practice, then the purpose of the Mahamudra practice is to realize the nature of the five negative thoughts or afflictive emotions as the five wisdoms. In Mahamudra we say, "Grant me blessings so that the confusion, the error may dawn as the wisdom awareness at once." So within that, for example, first strong desire, attachment, or strong hatred, at that time, see how your Mahamudra practice is. How much strength does your practice have? If you have the strength of the Mahamudra practice, you can handle them, these powerful thoughts of desire or hatred. And if you don't have it, then one loses against them. You get defeated. So it is a big battle.

In the fourth of the four empowerments there are teachings called, "introducing the nature of mind" which point out that this wisdom awareness is like the center of the space, like the vajra, or the center of the space-vajra. What that means is that the reality of the ultimate is free from all the boundaries and is of the nature of clarity. So that vajra is not just this metal thing that you see.

The vajra has a symbolic meaning. It is just a metaphor. The five points of the vajra are the five wisdoms, the five Buddhas, the lower five are the five female Buddhas. There are eight lotuses, upper and lower, which are the eight male and female Bodhisattvas. At the center is symbolized the inseparability of emptiness and compassion.

In the Vajrayana, there are a lot of names, which include the term vajra. There are "vajra master", "vajra disciple", "vajra enlightenment," "vajra hell." What these mean are that as soon as you realize the nature of the mind and the conceptual thoughts as Mahamudra, that realization is so powerful. It just destroys, in that moment, the strong concept of the attachment or hatred. In that very moment it liberates one to the enlightened state. So it destroys samsara, that's the meaning of vajra. But on the other hand, if we could not handle the thoughts well, by neglecting Mahamudra practice, then that vajra negative thought destroys the enlightenment, and draws one into the hell realms.

Therefore, when you practice Mahamudra, when people irritate you, don't hesitate to face this with Mahamudra practice. Instead just feel joy. "Oh, I am getting a good opportunity to test myself and whether my practice is good enough or not." Because if you just sit in the corner of a room in your house without anybody around, then you think, "Oh, my meditation is so wonderful! Really I am experiencing enlightenment." But as soon as someone comes along who agitates you, then there it comes again, that wrathful face! So see that nature.

In the case, for example, where you are in a house and there are people going back and forth and that irritates you, and somebody yells at you too, at all those times, right there and then just sustain the Mahamudra practice. And if you cannot sustain the Mahamudra practice, then you have to be ashamed of yourself. "Oh, I am not doing enough. What kind of Mahamudra practitioner am I?"

Generally, in a samsara state, these negative thoughts are the source of all the suffering. All the negative thoughts create all the negative karma. But in the Mahamudra practice itself, these thoughts are kind of supportive and useful. When there is a gigantic fire and then you throw more fuel on it, it burns with greater intensity and becomes even bigger. So when you practice Mahamudra, when negative thoughts arise, it makes the Mahamudra practice more effective and increase. So to do this, whether these conceptual thoughts, the attachment and hatred, liberate or do not liberate depends on how much we have established the meditation practice of Mahamudra. It depends on whether or not we have established the confidence in the practice. That is called "seeing the confusion dawn as wisdom."

For example, when such a strong hatred and anger arises in the mind, right at that moment, without any other choice, just seal that nature as the Mahamudra. Look at that Mahamudra nature. When one can do that it is called "the nature of the hatred is the mirror-like wisdom" and that is the Buddha Vajrasattva or the Buddha Akshobya. When a strong desire or attachment arises, right at that moment look at its nature and given no chance, see it by the Mahamudra meditation. When you transform it or see it to have the nature of Dharmakaya or Mahamudra it is called "the wisdom called discriminating wisdom" or Buddha Amitabha. And so forth. We can use, transform or see the nature of all of the five afflictive emotions as the five wisdoms. This is Mahamudra practice. [Garchen Rinpoche is offered and eats a piece of fruit. Khenpo: Ah, the fruit of Mahamudra!] The inseparability of appearance and emptiness is called the "vajra body" or vajra form, Buddha's wisdom body. Experiencing taste, the delicious taste in emptiness nature, is the vajra speech!

So with this meditation practice, the transformation which happens when realizing all as the Dharmakaya or Mahamudra nature is called "everything rises as the supporter of the meditation or supporting the meditation practice" whether it is positive or negative. It is like when an enemy really treats you so badly and at that time one thinks, "This is such a great spiritual master, evoking all of my problems and making them come out and enabling me to see the very naked nature of myself. So I have to deal with this, my own thoughts, and purify all this." Or if you see someone begging on the street, at that time, "Oh, this person is a subject of compassion, suffering, so this is also reminding me of my practice." Or if somebody like a friend comes and brings you gifts and say, "Oh, how wonderful you are," at that time, and you think, "Oh, this is a wonderful time to practice loving-kindness to all sentient beings." Or when you get sick, "Oh, this is also reminding me of my practice. For this I'm grateful. If everything goes well or works out perfectly, then I will have no idea or mind by which to practice the Dharma. By getting this sickness, this is so helpful for reminding me of my practice." We can continue like this, "May all sentient beings who are sick and who are suffering, may they be purified by this, by my very sickness. May I substitute this small sickness for all the suffering of sentient beings and their sicknesses. This is reminding me of my practice. I am so grateful."

So with regards to any people you meet, whether better off or worse off, whether educated or uneducated, there is always an opportunity to remember the practice in Mahamudra.

Since all sentient beings have Buddha nature and since Buddha's manifestation can be anywhere, in the human realm, in the animal realms, in the hungry ghost realm, in the hell realms, we cannot say that anyone is not a Buddha's emanation or manifestation. We cannot judge anybody. So from that point of view, we have to practice the pure vision. Who knows? This "anybody" who we encounter could be Buddha's emanation or a Bodhisattva's manifestation. "So I have to be careful. I have to watch my thought." Meditate on that. In that way, whatever positive thought arises, whatever negative thought arises, pacify them into the Mahamudra realization. Integrate them into the Mahamudra practice. In that way, all this visible appearance can be transformed into the all-pervading pure realm.

Ignorance and Sleep Dawning as Wisdom

With regards to transforming or seeing the five negative thoughts as the five wisdoms, we didn't talk much about ignorance. The significance of the ignorance is manifest in sleep. During sleep, you are just like dead. There is not any awareness. There is nothing at all. It is so difficult to bring any kind of practice in there during that time. There is one thing you can do before you go to sleep. This is called the "vajra recitation."

OM, AH, HUM. In your heart visualize the clarity nature as a light. Now you have to go to sleep because you have to work so hard, isn't that so? Without sleep you can't work. So breathe in OM, then with the wind or air inside there is AH, and when you breathe out, exhale, HUM. Just do this when you go to sleep. With that you will fall asleep. It is a great purification of the sleep and of the ignorance.

And then regarding the other negative thoughts, just when any negative thought arises, you just give it an "empowerment." When you give rise to hatred, you give it the empowerment of the mirror-like wisdom. When desire arises, give the empowerment of discriminating wisdom. When pride arises, give the empowerment of the equanimity wisdom. When jealousy arises, give the empowerment of the all-accomplishing wisdom. Give empowerment means transformation. So do like that.

Hesitation and Complete Confidence

Anyway, ignorance, confusion, and delusions are very profound! There are seven different types of ignorance including being forgetful, lack of clarity, agitated mind – moving around and always querying this or that, doubt, ignorance-itself, like this. All seven are not given here but of the seven types, the doubt or hesitation is one of the very great obstacles blocking the road to progress. When you meditate, it doesn't allow you to progress. To enhance your meditation practice, you have to have full confidence. This needs to be complete confidence, definitive. Like when you are completely sure you are doing the right thing. That kind of confidence is necessary. When you have that, on the basis of that, you will continue to progress. With hesitation, there is no more progress.

Therefore, yesterday I mentioned about the lineage from Vajradhara until now, and how in all of the lineage, there is no doubt. There is no doubt as to what Buddha taught and what Dharma teachings are all about. These Dharma teachings are so extremely pure and precious. There is no doubt about that.

We have to dispel all the doubts. And as long as there is a doubt regarding your instruction or in your meditation, "maybe this right", "maybe this not right", until you fix that, there is no progress. So when we say this is right or wrong, just say, "Oh, that is the doubt."

This doubt is called one of the maras to the meditation in that it creates obstacles. So this is the way to transform or carry or realize that the nature of the five negative are the five wisdoms. Just see, realize all of the five negative thoughts as the five wisdoms. This is done without any antidote, without remedy, by just realizing its own nature.

Realization of the One Meaning and the Five Wisdoms

So the five wisdoms are briefly mentioned here in this non-abiding Mahamudra tantra text. When you have the realization of the Mahamudra, that state of mind is so vast. It sees everything and dispels all delusions, the ignorance. That great appearance is called Vairochana. That is the very essence of Mahamudra. When you put it into practice, just sustain it, this clarity-emptiness nature, without moving from that state. That is the essence of all, there is no other than that. And that is called Akshobya. The vajra Akshobya. And in this realization of Mahamudra one has the control, the power to manifest all the wish-fulfilling jewels, all the supreme achievements. There is nothing higher to achieve. That is called Ratnasambhava. And from this one meaning, when you realize this one meaning, you know everything. And all the infinite qualities and experiences arise from that. That is called Amitabha. And when you have this one meaning, the realization of this co-emergent wisdom, all the activities are meaningful and are accomplished. That is called Amogasiddhi.

The King of Old Yogis

So this is the owner of all. This awareness, this mindfulness, is the owner. In samsara, we are lost, there is no owner, there is no one who takes care, and there is no one who is taken care of. But this is the way to take care. This is the owner.

Chenrezig said, "Whatever thought arises in the mind, that is the unborn, unchanging nature, and is no different from the Mahamudra. Whatever thought arises, if you just sustain the mindfulness state of the Mahamudra, then that itself, right where it is arising is the nature of emptiness." This is called "the king of the old yogis" and there is no doubt about that.

In this way it is so simple that sometimes you can't believe it. Just as any thought rises, look at it, it dissolves, that's it.

Sometimes here, because it is so simple, so easy, you don't trust it. We have such high expectations. "Oh, it must be so difficult, so concrete, somewhere there," like that. But you don't realize how simple it is. Just look at the mind, any thought arises, it dissolves. Then just sustain that. Meditate. So we just need the continuity of the mindfulness and awareness.

View, Meditation and Conduct – Advice for Various Levels

Now in the practice of Mahamudra, we have what are called the Mahamudra view, Mahamudra meditation, and Mahamudra conduct or how you behave. You look with the view of the Mahamudra, realize it and sustain it through meditation practice, and then to support that and to progress you need virtuous conduct.

So this depends on the individual. For example, for beginners we are to sustain that and meditate on impermanence, death. Everything has just a momentary nature. Everything is of a transitory nature. Everything is always changing. This is not just my belief. This is how it is, how everything happens. Reflect on the reality and rare opportunity of the precious human life, how difficult it is to achieve it, to have it. So like that, put emphasis on the mind, constantly. And then meditate and practice.

When our practice is more enhanced and has progressed further based on the awareness of impermanence and the precious human life, then practice Bodhicitta. Bodhicitta is the backbone of the Buddhism. In Bodhicitta, there's relative Bodhicitta and absolute Bodhicitta. Relative Bodhicitta is the very cause by which to actualize the ultimate Bodhicitta. Relative Bodhicitta is like the trunk of the tree and ultimate Bodhicitta is like the flowers or fruit on the tree. To enhance Bodhicitta practice, there is the practice of the six paramitas or six perfections. The six perfections are designed to gather great accumulations and accomplish all the purification of the obscurations and the negative karmas, and so forth. And through them, there is a greater chance of realizing Mahamudra.

In the practice of the six paramitas, there are two kinds of benefits, one in the temporary, relative state, one in the absolute state. In the relative state, by practicing generosity, we get a good condition, by practicing moral ethics, we get a good human life, by practicing patience, we get a positive surrounding, so enhance all of these qualities, perseverance, and so forth. For example, in the practice of generosity there are the practices of giving wealth, giving fearlessness, and giving Dharma teachings or sharing wisdom and skillful means. Sharing wisdom and skills are the most important gifts among all giving. So like this, in our daily life, we can be aware and put together or organize our life. Whether we are sitting, working, driving, in all of these there are practices that can be done.

And whether one is highly realized in the Mahamudra practice, or is just a beginner, whatever that person may be, the most important quality is perseverance or joyous effort. What joyous effort means is mindfulness and awareness. That is very, very important. The advancement of all of our meditation practice depends on the perseverance of the mindfulness.

Conclusion

The Practice of Realization

Now today we are here and you are here receiving these teachings. I am here, Khenpo is translating here, and all of this didn't just happen through coincidence, or through something intellectual. It happened through all the causes and conditions which we gathered through many lifetimes. So therefore these profound Mahamudra instructions were given.

I have had many relatives and very close friends, and have not given them these Mahamudra instructions. They didn't ask and so I didn't give them. Now here today I have given all this instruction, and you have gathered vast accumulation of merit and good karma by receiving this. What is most important now, upon receiving these teachings, is not to waste them. To make them useful and fruitful, we have to practice.

To do practice it is important to look at the life stories of the great masters in the past, such as those in the translation of *The Great Kagyü Masters*. Read their life stories and how they went through things. In particular, Milarepa's life story is so valuable and is available. It is so clear, so vivid, and everyone can comprehend and relate to it. So many people can do that. Milarepa's life story is so powerful, and is of such an uncontrived nature. It is not just something which is there intellectually. It is based on his experience, what he went through.

When I was in the labor camp, there was no access to books. All I had was Milarepa's life story. I just read it repeatedly, many times over and over again. Yet I could not read all the time, only during certain times. When you read Milarepa's life story, then you will see the qualities of Milarepa. The pictures of Milarepa appear so vividly to our minds. It is so clear, how he went though things, how he meditated, how he actualized realization, and how he benefited sentient beings.

With this, if you do Mahamudra practice, all your doubts and obstacles will be dispelled. Even if sometimes it is not possible to dispel obstacles in that moment, if that is not accomplished, then it definitely will happen after a few days. Just recollect Milarepa, and meditate on that.

Milarepa himself said, "I went through great hardship, and realized the total nature of the Vajradhara. In the future, if followers think of me, they will not face these obstacles." Since he attained complete enlightenment, Buddhahood is like the four elements in that it pervades to all, to every sentient being. His wisdom and compassion are there so clearly.

Therefore, first get the understanding and realization of Mahamudra. Then, to enhance your progress, devotion to the lama is so powerful, so important. Without it, it enhancement is not possible.

A teacher once sent several of his monks to receive teachings from a great Khenpo with emphasis on getting teachings on the nature of mind. When the monks got there they discovered that they could not communicate well because of the language barriers. Still they sat there with devotion and confidence during instruction. Without much understanding of the words, they completely received all of the transmission and came back and said, "We understood. We didn't understand a word of what he said, but we understood the meaning, what it was all about. We realized it."

It is like your mind and the lama's mind. In nature, there is no difference. When you recognize your own mind then there is no difference between your mind and the lama's mind, that which you receive. It is like electricity. In the light of the United States, the light of China, or the light of anywhere, there is only light. There is no difference. There are different locations, but as far as the nature of light goes, there is no difference.

To actualize this Mahamudra do Guru yoga, meditate on receiving blessings, and meditate on Mahamudra. Get the confidence through the lineage and root lamas and through the teachings. With that, if one does the meditation there is no doubt that one will experience Mahamudra realization.

So there are some other different teachings which are helpful.

In the Sakya teachings there are the four renunciations or "four free-from-the-attachments." If one attaches to this life, one is not a Dharma practitioner; if one attaches to samsara, there is no renunciation; if one attaches to oneself, there is no Bodhicitta; if one attaches to the grasping, there is no view.

In addition, there are the three very important points of the Drukpa Kagyü. Tilopa said there were three essential points. At the outset, put importance on Guru yoga; to dispel the obstacles and realize into the Dharmakaya, there is Guru yoga; to enhance the meditation into

Dharmakaya, there is Guru yoga. So what that means is you don't have to see the lama as if "he is outside there" and that "I am inside here." When you have mindfulness and awareness, then that's the lama. That is inseparability from the lama. Jigme Lingpa said this.

When you do Milarepa Guru Yoga and he dissolves into you, meditate on that. Say to yourself, "I receive Milarepa. He dissolve into me. My awareness, mindfulness, is not different from Milarepa's." Sustain that, meditate on that. Or like when you do Lord Jigten Sumgön Guru Yoga and he dissolves into you, meditate, "I am no different than Lord Jigten Sumgön's wisdom and mindfulness." Just sustain that, just do that kind of meditation practice.

In that way you don't have to feel distance between the lama and yourself. He is just within you always. So you don't have to think, "Oh, my lama is too far. I can't get there. What should I do?" Wherever you are, there is the lama.

When we have that continuity of the mindfulness and awareness, which is inseparable from the lama, there is the quality called "chökur tigle ngetse(?)" [Khenpo: I don't know how to translate that. Who can help me?], perhaps "Dharmakaya, one-point". So this is one-point, basically absolute reality. We should not feel that this one point, Dharmakaya is something out there. That very mindfulness, inseparable from the lama, that is the Dharmakaya. Right there is all of the essence.

First recognize that, then sustain that with the devotion to the lama, like Milarepa, Jigten Sumgön, all those lamas. Do those practices well and receive those blessings. Devotion is so powerful. It kind of dispels all the obstacles. It softens the mind which is so rigid, arrogant. The arrogance and rigidity dissolve. They are softened by devotion to the lama.

Then practice Bodhicitta. Bodhicitta is releasing self-grasping, self-cherishing. Also, of course, calmly abiding or shamatha, is very important. So when you have these supports, these practices, without much difficulty, one will realize one's own mind. When realizing this, one's mind is free from all the doubt and hesitation. Just continue there, in that. And then to sustain it and to enhance it, also, place importance also on the other practices.

I will do the Mahamudra meditation every day, every morning, and every evening, and think of you all. Everybody will be put in under the umbrella of my Mahamudra meditation. So if you do these things and practice on a regular basis and practice in this way then there is the opportunity to unify our realization of Mahamudra [Khenpo: Rinpoche and yours.]

So there may come a time when you may ask, "What is the sign of accomplishing this Mahamudra practice, perhaps clairvoyance, perhaps levitation?" The great Khenpo Rinpoche from whom I received teachings said things like clairvoyance, levitation, and so forth are not the qualities of Mahamudra. The most important sign of realizing Mahamudra is compassion. The more there is compassion in the mind, the more it enhances itself, and that is the sign of the arising of Mahamudra realization.

Printed in Poland
by Amazon Fulfillment
Poland Sp. z o.o., Wrocław
16 May 2021

bdcb2fb1-5004-47c5-ae5a-30e6a764ec89R01